The Old Testament
Books Made
SIMPLE

Everything You Should
Have Learned
in Sunday School
(and Probably Didn't)

James E. Smith

1959 ★ 2009
COLLEGE
P R E S S

International Standard Book Number: 978-0-89900-991-9

Dedicated to
Malcolm & Loraine Odham
Friends
and
Fellow Servants

CONTENTS

PREFACE

This is the second volume in the *Made Simple* series. It is recommended that the student first study the volume entitled, *Bible History Made Simple*. Once you have learned the time line for biblical history, the major characters and events, then you are ready to take a closer look at the individual books of the Bible.

The structure of the chapters in this book is derived from the account of the call of Samuel. The Lord called to Samuel three times in the night. Each time the boy thought that it was Eli who was calling. Finally the old priest realized that it must be the Lord who was calling to Samuel in the night. Eli instructed Samuel to respond to the next call with these words: *Speak, LORD, for your servant hears* (1 Samuel 3:9).

Eli's advice to Samuel is appropriate for all students of God's word. As we approach the pages of the holy book we need to be asking God to speak to us. He speaks to us through his word. We, on our part, must be ready to hear what he has to say.

The letters of the word SPEAKS are used to outline the discussion of each Old Testament book. **S** = Situation — the background of the book is set forth. **P** = Plan — book organization is discussed. **E** = Eternal Purpose — the immediate and ultimate purposes for each book are set forth. **A** = Anticipation — how the book anticipates the coming of Christ. **K** = Keys — the key chapter, verse, phrases, and words in the book are identified. **S** = Special Features — a list of oddities, peculiarities, or facts that point to the uniqueness of each book.

God *SPEAKS* in his word. We must *HEAR*. The discussion of each book has a section entitled HEAR. This section contains a sampling of the outstanding chapters and verses in each book. Serious students will want to read at least the key chapter for each book, and the outstanding chapters when they are identified.

I have utilized the King James Version (modernized) throughout unless otherwise indicated.

James E. Smith
Florida Christian College

CHAPTER ONE

TOURING THE LIBRARY

Picture a library complex consisting of two buildings with a courtyard separating them. The older books in the library's collection are housed in the first building. The books in the first building range from 2400 to 3800 years old. Across the courtyard in the second building the newer books are housed. They, too, are now very old. These "newer" books are approaching 2,000 years of age. In this chapter we want to take a tour of the first building of our imaginary library.

Christians refer to the books housed in the first building of the imaginary library as the *Old Testament*. There are thirty-nine valuable books in this building. For Jews these books constitute the entire Bible, which they call *Tanak*. The consonants of this term (*T N K*) refer to the three major sections into which the Jews organize the books in their sacred library: *T = Torah (law)*, the Jewish name for the first five books (Genesis, Exodus, Leviticus, Numbers, Deuteronomy); *N = Nebhiim (Prophets)*, the Jewish name for eight books (Joshua, Judges, Samuel, Kings, Isaiah, Jeremiah, Ezekiel, the Twelve). *K= Kethubim (Writings)*, the rest of the books of the Old Testament.

Jews count only 22 or 24 books in their biblical library. They combine several of the 39 books that Christians count in their Old Testament. Here, however, is the bottom line: The 22 or 24 books counted by the Jews in their Bible are the same as the 39 books that Christians count in their Old Testament. Christians believe that God delivered his oracles or Scriptures to the Jews (Romans 3:2). So only the books accepted by the Jews as Scripture were included by the Christians as part of their Bible. Furthermore, most of these books were cited by Christ and the apostles in such a way as to indicate that they were to be received as Scripture by Christians.

The Old Testament books describe God's choice of a special people through whom he planned one day to bring his Son into the world. Within the Old Testament library there is a variety of literature. Here one finds history, law, poetry, wisdom literature, worship literature, and predictive material, just to name a few categories.

Here are some interesting facts about the Old Testament:

- ❖ **Consists of 39 books.**
- ❖ **Written by at least 32 writers.**
- ❖ **Took about 1,000 years to write.**
- ❖ **Covers at least 3800 years of history.**
- ❖ **Makes up 77% of the Bible.**
- ❖ **Contains 929 chapters; 23,214 verses.**

Overview of the Old Testament

Now let's look more closely at some of the points listed above.

Writers

Christians believe that God is the ultimate Author of all Scripture (2 Timothy 3:16). He guided the various human writers so that what they wrote reflected exactly what God wanted people to know. This guiding process is called *inspiration*. Through his Holy Spirit God exerted his influence over the writers (2 Peter 1:21) so that they were guided into all truth (John 16:13). Because the writers received supernatural assistance in their writing, Christians believe that the writings of Scripture are *inerrant*, i.e., without error.

God used about 32 human writers to produce the books of the Old Testament. The names of some of these writers are rather famous. You may have heard of Moses, David, and Solomon. The names of other writers are not so well known. Have you heard of Ezra? Of Amos? Of Agur?

Some of the writers contributed multiple books to the collection. Moses wrote five, possibly six, of the Old Testament books. Solomon wrote three books, Jeremiah at least two. Sixteen writers contributed but one book to the collection. Some of the books have contributions from multiple writers. A number of the Old Testament books are written anonymously.

Time Frame

When considering the matter of chronology, two issues must be considered separately. First, how old are the *books* of the Old Testament? This issue might be designated *literary time*. Second, how much time is covered in the history reported in the Old Testament? This issue might be designated *historical time*.

The oldest books of the Old Testament were written by Moses just before 1400 BC. These books are Genesis, Exodus, Leviticus, Numbers, and Deuteronomy. Ancient tradition also attributed the Book of Job to Moses. The latest books of the Old Testament were written just before 400 BC. These are the books of Ezra, Nehemiah, Esther, and Malachi. So the writing of the Old Testament took about 1,000 years.

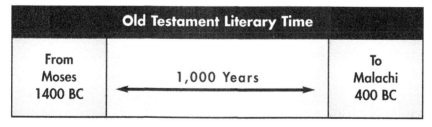

Old Testament Literary Time		
From Moses 1400 BC	←——— 1,000 Years ———→	To Malachi 400 BC

While the Old Testament contains sermons, proverbs, hymns, prophecies, and laws, it also tells a story. In fact, that story or history is the framework without which nothing else in the Old Testament makes sense. This framework is present primarily in the following books: Genesis, Exodus 1–19, Numbers 10–14 + 16–17 + 20–27 + 31–33, Joshua, Judges, Ruth, 1 & 2 Samuel, 1 & 2 Kings, 1 & 2 Chronicles, Ezra, Nehemiah, and Esther. This constitutes about 37% of the Old Testament.

In reading through this material one must distinguish between *forward motion books* and *sidestep or spotlight books.* For the most part the historical books of the Old Testament tell their story in chronological order. There are, however, three major exceptions. The last six chapters of Judges + Ruth do not move the history forward. The same is true of 1 & 2 Chronicles and Esther. This material must be "plugged in" to the historical framework established by the forward motion books. Let's illustrate:

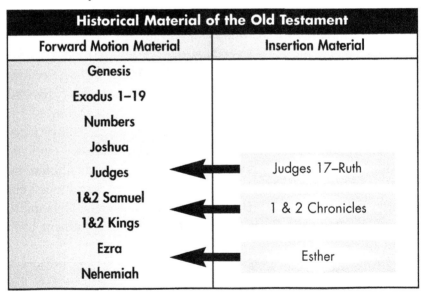

Most Bible scholars do not attempt to put dates on the events of Genesis prior to Abraham. From biblical data the birth of Abraham can be placed at about 2165 BC. For the purposes of simplicity, this figure can be rounded off to 2000 BC.

The last dateable event of the Old Testament is the second governorship of Nehemiah (Nehemiah 13). This can be dated to about 432 BC. This number can be rounded off to 400 BC. So the dateable history related in the Old Testament covers at least 1600 years.

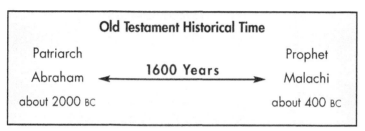

Importance of the Old Testament

Why should a Christian be interested in the Old Testament? This is a fair question. It deserves a forthright answer. There are at least twelve good reasons why every Christian should be acquainted with the contents of the Old Testament.

1. The Old Testament constitutes the first great portion of the revelation of God to man. By its very nature divine revelation is permanent. God spoke in many different ways to the saints of old through the prophets (Hebrews 1:1). The methods of revelation changed, as did the commandments of God and the symbolism; but the revelation itself was intended to do its work in the hearts of men through the ages.

2. The Old Testament begins with the declaration *in the beginning God created the heavens and the earth* (Genesis 1:1). The existence of the one true and living God is the first principle of true religion. Our dependence upon the Creator and our accountability to him are made crystal clear in the older Testament.

3. The Old Testament offers lengthy discussion of some of the most challenging questions of life: Why do good people suffer? (Job) What is the meaning of life? (Ecclesiastes) Where did we come from? (Genesis) How can I get along with those around me? (Proverbs) How can I know if I'm in love? (Song of Solomon)

4. The opening chapters of Genesis constitute the historic seed plot of the whole divine plan of human redemption.

5. The Old Testament contains an authoritative account of salvation history through the Patriarchal and Mosaic ages of time. Without the older Testament the believer will lack perspective. Only those who have looked upon the awesome sweep of Genesis to the Gospels and the Revelation can hope to glimpse the range and scope of God's redemptive purpose.

6. It is impossible to understand the New Testament accurately without a grasp of the Old Testament. In many cases the New Testament writers assume a prior knowledge of Old Testament concepts as they discuss matters like atonement and holiness.

7. The Old Testament contains many fundamental principles that are still as true today as the day they were written.

8. The Old Testament contains an abundance of rich biographical material that illustrates, motivates, warns, and challenges Christians. Close the Old Testament and you shut yourself off from the spiritual biographies of men and women whose experiences with God offer rich and practical instruction.

9. Much helpful devotional material will be found throughout the Old Testament, especially in the Psalms. Without the Old Testament the Christian is deprived of rich resources for worship and prayer.

10. In the Old Testament we see the gospel of Christ in preview, promise, and prophecy. No person can intelligently make the confession that Jesus is the Christ without some knowledge of Old Testament prophecies that predict the details of his life.

11. The New Testament encourages Christians to learn from events in the Old Testament. See 1 Corinthians 10:11 and Romans 4:22-25.

12. The example of the use of the Old Testament by Jesus and his apostles encourages Christians to pursue the study of this portion of God's word.

Organization of the Old Testament

Like the books of a library, the thirty-nine books of the Old Testament are organized into four major sections: Foundation Books, Framework Books, Faith Books and Focus Books. Let's look briefly at each of these sections.

Foundation Books

The first five books of the Old Testament are sometimes called the Books of Law; but they contain much more than legal material. Jews refer to these books as the *Torah,* a term that means *teaching, instruction,* or *law.* An ancient name for these five books in Christian circles is *Pentateuch,* a term that means *five scrolls.*

First Section of the Biblical Library *Foundation Books*				
1 Genesis	**2** Exodus	**3** Leviticus	**4** Numbers	**5** Deuteronomy
Gen/Gn	Exod/Ex	Lev/Lv	Num/Nm	Deut/Dt
History	History & Law	Law	Law & History	Law

The traditional view of the church and the Jewish authorities as well is that Moses is the author of these first five books. In dozens of verses the Pentateuch *claims* that Moses is the author. Other Old Testament books *concur* in this assignment. Mosaic authorship is *confirmed* by Christ and the apostles.

The Christ-link of the first five books is this: *Foundation for Christ.* These books lay the foundation for the coming of Christ in four ways:

❖ **Promises**

❖ **Prefigurements**

❖ **Precepts**

❖ **Prophecies**

Throughout the first five books God made *promises* to various individuals. Many of those promises have implications for mankind in general. God's initial blessing of Adam implies that mankind will be fruitful and multiply (Genesis 1:28). God promised Noah as representative of the human race that *"as long as the earth endures, seedtime and harvest, cold and heat, summer and winter, day and night will never cease"* (Genesis 8:22). God promised Abraham that through one of his descendants all nations of the earth would one day be blessed (Genesis 12:3).

Prefigurements are actions that display in some manner the principles of the spiritual truths of the Christian Age. The sacrificial rituals described in Leviticus and Numbers have as their long-range goal depicting the final sacrifice of Christ on the cross. Some of the historical events narrated in the first five books are interpreted in the New Testament as illustrations of present-day spiritual principles. For example, the great Flood of Noah's day is said by the Apostle Peter to be an illustration of baptism (1 Peter 3:21). Some of the individuals who appear in the first five books prefigure Christ. For example, Melchizedek, the king of Salem and priest of the Most High (Genesis 14:18-20) prefigures Christ as our king and high priest.

The *precepts* or laws recorded in the Pentateuch were designed to prepare the world for the coming of Christ. God's Law reveals the sinfulness of man; it demonstrates man's need for God's grace and mercy.

The five foundational books contain several specific *predictions* that Christians think are the earliest announcements of the coming of Christ. The first such prediction (Genesis 3:15) announces that one born of woman ultimately will crush the head of Serpent (Satan). Jacob predicted that Shiloh, the Rest-bringer, will come to establish a glorious kingdom (Genesis 49:10). Balaam spoke of him as the Star and Scepter (Numbers 24:17-19) who will defeat the enemies of God's people. Moses announced that God will raise up a prophet like himself (Deuteronomy 18:17-19).

Framework Books

The next shelf in the biblical library contains twelve volumes. These are frequently called the *Historical Books*. The designation *Framework* indicates that these books describe the history of God's people from the death of Moses to the death of Malachi (about 1,000 years). The rest of the books of the Old Testament fit into this historical framework at various points.

Section Two of the Biblical Library *Framework Books*					
History before the Kings		History during the Kings		History after the Kings	
Joshua (Josh)	Judges (Judg)	1&2 Samuel (Sam/Sm)	1&2 Kings (Kgs)	Ezra	Nehemiah (Neh)
Ruth		1&2 Chronicles (Chron/Chr)		Esther (Esth)	

The Framework Books are anonymous. Jewish tradition assigns these books to eight different writers: Joshua, Samuel, Gad, Nathan, Jeremiah, Ezra, Nehemiah and Mordecai.

The Christ-link for the twelve Framework Books is **Preparation for Christ**. These twelve books cover a history of roughly a thousand years, from the death of Moses (ca. 1400 BC) to the death of Malachi (ca. 400 BC). They report how God worked with the nation Israel over this period to shape a remnant that was prepared to recognize Christ when he appeared.

There are four major emphases in the Framework Books. First, God is faithful to his promises to Abraham and to David. Second, the prophets are God's ambassadors sent from the Great King to hold his people accountable for observing God's covenant. Third, God's earthly dwelling was first in the Tabernacle, then in the Temple. Fourth, faithfulness to the Lord is the single standard by which all leaders of Israel were measured.

Faith Books

The Faith Books of the Old Testament are five in number—Job, Psalms, Proverbs, Ecclesiastes, and Song of Songs (or Song of Solomon). These books focus on individuals. They are sometimes called Devotional Books or Poetic Books or Experiential Books. This section explores how the faith of individual believers expresses itself in a variety of circumstances.

Section Three of Biblical Library *Faith Books*				
Job	Psalms	Proverbs	Ecclesiastes	Song of Solomon
	Ps/Pss	Prov	Eccl	S. of Sol
Wisdom Lit.	Worship Lit.	Wisdom Lit.	Wisdom Lit.	Wisdom Lit.

Most of the material in the Faith Books was written about a thousand years before Christ. David and his son Solomon were the major contributors. Solomon wrote the Song, most of Proverbs, and probably Ecclesiastes. Solomon included a few sayings of Agur and a King Lemuel in the Book of Proverbs. David wrote at least seventy-five of the psalms. Asaph, Heman, Jeduthan, and the sons of Korah were Levites living at the time of David/Solomon who contributed to the Book of Psalms. Psalm 90 is attributed to Moses. Fifty psalms are anonymous, but many of them were probably written by David. Job is anonymous. Jewish tradition assigns the Book of Job to Moses; but many modern scholars think Job was written during the time of Solomon.

The Christ-link for the Faith Books is *Aspiration for Christ*. The only book of the five that has significant messianic prophecy is Psalms. David was a prophet. He wrote of Christ in at least thirteen psalms. For the most part the rest of the psalms, and the other four Faith Books express longings or aspirations that ultimately were fulfilled in Christ. Job, for example, expresses the desire for a mediator or go-between to stand between himself and God. Christ is that mediator (1 Timothy 2:5).

Focus Books

The last seventeen books of the Old Testament are prophetic books. They focus on national issues that arose in various periods of the history of Israel. These issue-oriented books again have been broken down into two subgroups according to size. The five larger focus books are often called the Major Prophets.

Section Four of the Biblical Library *Larger Focus Books*				
Isaiah	Jeremiah	Lamentations	Ezekiel	Daniel
Isa	Jer	Lam	Ezek	Dan
Announcement of Jerusalem Destruction		Description of Jerusalem Destruction	Implications of Jerusalem Destruction	

The five books of Major Prophets were written by four great prophets. The five poems that constitute the Book of Lamentations were written by Jeremiah to express sorrow over the destruction of Jerusalem in 586 BC. In fact, early in the history of the Bible, the Book of Lamentations seems to have been an appendix to the Book of Jeremiah.

Isaiah and Jeremiah had long ministries in Jerusalem; Ezekiel and Daniel had long ministries in Babylon. Isaiah and Jeremiah prophesied mostly before the destruction of Jerusalem (586 BC); Ezekiel and Daniel prophesied immediately before and for several years after the destruction of Jerusalem.

The twelve smaller focus books are frequently called Minor Prophets. The best way to learn the names of the Minor Prophets is by groups of three.

Section Five of the Biblical Library *Smaller Focus Books*			
Hosea Joel Amos	Obadiah Jonah Micah	Nahum Habakkuk Zephaniah	Haggai Zechariah Malachi

The twelve Minor Prophets are more like pamphlets than books. In fact, because of their size the Jews lump them all together and count them as one book, which they call The Twelve. The nature of the material contained in the Minor Prophets resembles that of the Major Prophets. The issues of concern, however, may be different because some of the Minor Prophets lived in different historical periods.

Although the books of the Minor Prophets follow the Major Prophets in the Bible, the ministries of these prophets do not chronologically follow the ministries of Isaiah, Jeremiah, Ezekiel, and Daniel. Four of the Minor Prophets (Obadiah, Joel, Jonah, Amos) preceded Isaiah, earliest of the Major Prophets. Hosea and Micah were contemporary with Isaiah. Two Minor Prophets (Nahum, Zephaniah) preached between the ministries of Isaiah and Jeremiah. Habakkuk's ministry overlapped that of Jeremiah. Three Minor Prophets (Haggai, Zechariah, Malachi) prophesied after Daniel, the last of the Major Prophets. For the present do not concern yourself about the relationship of these ministries except for this one fact: *the Minor Prophets do not appear in the Bible in chronological order.*

So the picture looks like this. Read the following chart from top to bottom and from left to right, with the earliest prophetic books to the left. Capital letters are the Major Prophets. It is not important for now that you know the prophets in chronological order. We will place them in the proper periods of Old Testament history later.

	ISAIAH	JEREMIAH	DANIEL EZEKIEL	
Obadiah Joel Jonah Amos	Hosea Micah	Nahum Zephaniah Habakkuk		Haggai Zechariah Malachi

You have now completed your tour of the Old Testament library. We have seen that the books are placed in four sections that we called Foundation Books, Framework Books, Faith Books, and Focus Books. The fourth section is subdivided into two shelves. The first Focus shelf contains the larger books by the Major Prophets. The second shelf contains the pamphlet-sized books by the Minor Prophets.

CHAPTER TWO

FOUNDATION BOOKS (1)
Genesis–Exodus

The first five books of the Bible form a distinct division of the biblical library. Jews refer to these five books as the *Torah* or *law*. At every synagogue service prescribed selections of these five books are read. For the Jews these five books are regarded as the holiest of the books of their Bible (our Old Testament). Among Christian scholars the first five books are generally called the *Pentateuch*, which means *five scrolls*. When the New Testament references these books, it uses such titles as *law of Moses* (Luke 24:44), *Moses* (Luke 24:27; John 5:46), *writings of Moses* (John 5:46-47), or *word of God* (Mark 7:13).

Modern critics regard the Pentateuch as the product of anonymous authors living centuries apart. They charge that these five books are full of contradictions and errors. The New Testament titles mentioned in the previous paragraph, however, affirm that these books were the product of Moses. The majority of Christians throughout the world continue to believe and maintain that the Pentateuch is not a late, anonymous, untrustworthy compilation. These are the five books of Moses, the great lawgiver and prophet of God.

Bookwise the Pentateuch begins with Genesis and ends with Deuteronomy. Eventwise these books cover biblical history from creation to the death of Moses. Since most biblical scholars do not attempt to date creation, it is impossible to determine how many years are covered in these books. It can be determined from biblical data, however, that the death of Moses occurred about 1407 BC. Characterwise the Pentateuch begins with Adam and ends with Moses.

1ˢᵗ Bible Book
Book of Genesis
Patriarchs and Promises

Genesis is the seventh largest book in the Old Testament. It contains 50 chapters, 1,527 verses, and 32,267 words. In Jewish circles the first book of the Bible is sometimes called *Bereshith* (*b-ray'-sheath*), the first word in the Hebrew Bible. This word is translated *in the beginning*. The name *Genesis* comes from the ancient Greek and Latin Bibles. This is an appropriate name for the first book of the Bible. *Genesis* means *origin, birth, generation, beginning*.

Situation

After the long Egyptian bondage, God's people needed to be reminded of their roots—their heritage—and the promises God had made to their fathers. Some think that Moses wrote Genesis while he was still in Egypt before he fled for his life to the land of Midian (Exodus 2:15). If this is the case, then Genesis was written about 1490 BC. It is more likely, however, that Moses wrote this book during the forty years that he led the Israelites through the wilderness. This means that the book was written about 1425 BC.

Genesis makes no specific claim of authorship. From the earliest times, however, this book has been considered part of a five-volume set called the *Pentateuch*. The other four books of this collection make numerous claims that God spoke to and through Moses.

Plan

Genesis can be summed up in the words *patriarchs and promises*. The book focuses on the fathers of the Israelite nation and the promises that God made to them. The material is well-organized from several points of view.

Literary plan. Genesis has been organized in two main divisions. Chapters 1–11 offer the only authoritative account of the beginnings of the created world. In these chapters Moses describes four pivotal events: creation, the Fall of man into sin, the Flood of Noah's day, and the dispersion of mankind at the tower of Babel. In chapters 12–50 Moses relates the beginnings of the chosen people, the Israelites. In these chapters there are four pivotal characters — four generations of the same family: Abraham, Isaac, Jacob, and Joseph.

Moses has inserted into the Genesis storyline fragments of a long genealogy at eleven different places. These fragments serve as bridges from one part of the story to its sequel. In Hebrew the word *toledoth* (*toh-lay-dohth'*) is used to mark these genealogical fragments. *Toledoth* is translated *generations* in KJV, *account* in NIV. Clearly Moses intended the word *toledoth* to signal divisions of his work.

Spiritual plan. A spiritual structure to Genesis can also be discerned. Chapters 1–11 trace the *degeneration* of mankind in individuals (ch. 3), a family (ch. 4), society (ch. 6), and the nations (ch. 11). Chapters 12–50 trace God's plan for *regeneration* (renewal; new birth) in individuals (12:1–35:21); a family (35:22–38:29); in society (39:1–50:21); and in a nation (50:22-26).

Chronological plan. Genesis reports three periods of Old Testament history, and the beginning of a fourth period. The period from creation to the Flood is called the Beginnings Period (Genesis 1–9). From the Flood to the Call of Abraham is called the Scattering Period (Genesis 10–11). The duration of these first two periods of biblical history cannot be determined. From the Call of Abraham to the *Eisodus* — the going down into Egypt — is called the Pilgrim Period (Genesis 12–45). From the *Eisodus* to the death of Joseph is the first seventy years of the Egyptian Period (Genesis 46–50).

Geographical plan. Genesis focuses on three key areas. The venue of the first eleven chapters is the Fertile Crescent, that arc-shaped region stretching from the northern shore of the Persian Gulf to the borders of Egypt. Chapters 12–36 unfold for the most part in the land of Canaan. The land of Egypt is the venue for Genesis 37–50. Three key journeys are reported in Genesis: Abraham's journey from Ur (southern Iraq) to Canaan (Genesis 12), the journeys of Abraham, Isaac, and Jacob throughout the land of Canaan (Genesis 13–36), and the journey of the family of Jacob from Canaan to Egypt (Genesis 46).

Eternal Purpose

If one thinks of the great themes of the Bible as streams, the headwaters of those streams arise in Genesis. This book begins with creation. It answers the age-old questions, "Where did we come from?" and "Why are we here?" Genesis takes us back beyond recorded history. It reveals the origin both of the universe and of the human race. Genesis teaches that to understand who we are and where we came from we must begin with God.

Genesis ends with a coffin (figuratively speaking) — the coffin of Joseph. The note of Joseph's death ominously hints at the status of Israel at the beginning of the Book of Exodus, namely bondage. Moses wrote Genesis in order to remind the Israelites that God had promised to deliver them from bondage and give them the land of Canaan (Genesis 15:16; 46:4).

The larger purpose of the book is to set forth the promise that through a descendant of Abraham all nations of the earth one day will be blessed (Genesis 12:3; 18:18; 22:18; 28:14).

Genesis stresses that through faith man relates to his Creator. Faith is a fundamental principle of life. Failure in faith is failure in life. Genesis illustrates that faith may differ in expression. In Abraham faith manifested itself in obedience. Faith manifested itself in Isaac's patient interaction with adversaries. In Jacob faith manifested itself in a radical transformation of character.

Anticipation

Genesis contains four great announcements that specifically point forward to the coming of Messiah. First, Messiah will come from the seed of woman. He will crush the head of Satan (Genesis 3:15). Second, Messiah will come from the race of Shem, for God will dwell in the tents of Shem (Genesis 9:26). Unfortunately the true significance of this prediction has been blurred by the translation of the NIV. Third, Messiah will come from the seed of Abraham, Isaac, and Jacob. All nations will be blessed through this Promised Seed (Genesis 12:3; 26:4; 28:14). Fourth, Messiah will come from the tribe of Judah. He will usher in a peaceful and prosperous age (Genesis 49:10).

Genesis is also full of typology. A type is a person, place, object, or event that God designed to be a preview of coming events in the Christian Age. Each type has a corresponding antitype that is identified in the New Testament. This means that we are to look for correspondence between the type and the antitype. In Genesis there are four major types.

- ❖ **Adam (Romans 5:14):** a picture of Christ as head of a new creation.
- ❖ **Melchizedek (Hebrews 7:3):** a picture of Christ's priesthood.
- ❖ **Flood (1 Peter 3:21):** a picture of baptism.
- ❖ **Isaac (Hebrews 11:19):** a picture of Christ's resurrection.

Keys

The key chapter in the Book of Genesis is chapter 15. In this chapter God ratifies the covenant that he made with Abraham when he brought him into the land of Canaan. That covenant involved three major promises: *progeny, position,* and *possession.*

Abraham was seventy-five and childless when God promised that he was to have a son. He waited in faith another twenty-five years before the child of promise was finally born.

God promised that the descendants of Abraham were to be blessed and were to be a blessing (Genesis 12:2). They were to have a special *position* in respect to God. The descendants of Abraham eventually became the nation Israel. God chose Israel to be a priestly nation to intercede for all other nations.

God also promised Abraham a *possession*—the land of Canaan (Genesis 12:7).

The key verses in Genesis are these: *The LORD had said to Abram, "Leave your country, your people and your father's household and go to the land I will show you. ²I will make you into a great nation and I will bless you; I will make your name great, and you will be a blessing"* (Genesis 12:1-2). Abram (later called Abraham) was called by God to leave his homeland in Ur in southern Mesopotamia (modern Iraq). These verses mark the beginning of God's program of redemption through the descendants of Abraham.

In Genesis certain phrases appear frequently. The phrase *these are the generations of* appears eleven times in the book. The phrase *son of* is used in Genesis some twenty times.

The key words in the book are various forms of *bless*, which appear seventy-seven times. The word *die* or *died* appears in Genesis fifty-seven times.

Special Features

Four facts related to Genesis are worthy of special mention:

❖ Genesis provides a historical perspective for the rest of the Bible by covering more time than all the other biblical books combined.

❖ The first three chapters of Genesis are essential to a proper understanding of the last three chapters of Revelation.

❖ At least five ancient documents have turned up that reference a great flood in the ancient world, thus substantiating the Genesis account.

❖ God seems to champion the underdog throughout Genesis. Firstborn sons were passed over in favor of younger sons; at least three ladies—Sarah, Rebekah, and Rachel—were delivered from the ancient stigma of childlessness.

HEAR

God speaks in Genesis! We must hear! Here are some outstanding chapters for getting started in reading Genesis.

❖ How did it all begin? (Genesis 1)
❖ How did we get into this mess? (Genesis 3)
❖ Flood, ark, and rainbow (Genesis 6–9)
❖ Why do we speak different languages? (Genesis 11)
❖ Why is Israel special to God? (Genesis 12)
❖ What does God think of immorality? (Genesis 19)
❖ How does God fulfill his promises? (Genesis 21)
❖ How does faith reveal itself? (Genesis 22)
❖ Choosing the right wife (Genesis 24)
❖ Faith is living without scheming (Genesis 27)
❖ Encouragement in time of uncertainty (Genesis 28)
❖ God blesses those who yield to him (Genesis 32)
❖ Blessing in spite of mistreatment (Genesis 37)
❖ Planning wisely for disaster (Genesis 41)

Here are a few of the favorite lines from Genesis:

❖ *"This is now bone of my bones and flesh of my flesh; she shall be called 'woman,' for she was taken out of man"* (Genesis 2:23).
❖ *"You will not surely die," the serpent said to the woman* (Genesis 3:4).
❖ *"Am I my brother's keeper?"* (Genesis 4:9).
❖ *Noah found favor in the eyes of the LORD* (Genesis 6:8).
❖ *"I have set my rainbow in the clouds, and it will be the sign of the covenant between me and the earth"* (Genesis 9:13).
❖ *Abram believed the LORD; and he credited it to him as righteousness* (Genesis 15:6).
❖ *Is anything too hard for the LORD?* (Genesis 18:14).
❖ *"God himself will provide the lamb for the burnt offering"* (Genesis 22:8).
❖ *"Give me children, or I'll die!"* (Genesis 30:1).

❖ *"How then could I do such a wicked thing and sin against God?"* (Genesis 39:9).

❖ *"You intended to harm me, but God intended it for good to accomplish what is now being done, the saving of many lives"* (Genesis 50:20).

2nd Bible Book

Book of Exodus
Plagues and Precepts

Exodus is the sixth largest book of the Old Testament. It contains forty chapters organized into 1,207 verses—a total of 32,692 words. Jewish tradition uses the first two Hebrew words of the book for a title: *Ve'elleh Shemoth = And these are the names.* The title *Exodus (the way out)* comes from the Greek and Latin Bibles.

The importance of Exodus in the sacred collection is indicated by the degree to which it is cited in subsequent biblical literature. Hebrew poets and prophets quote Exodus and make use of its lessons of deliverance, faith, and hope, in their songs and prophecies. Likewise, New Testament writers frequently allude to the contents of this book. Exodus has been a source of inspiration for both Jews and Christians throughout the ages.

Situation

The contents of Exodus claim to have been given by God to Moses (Exodus 24:4). The book reflects a detailed, firsthand knowledge of events and places connected with Israel's exodus from Egypt. Exodus was probably written about 1444 BC while the people of Israel were wandering in the vast wilderness east of Egypt.

Exodus begins with a brief recapitulation of Genesis 46. This shows that Moses intended Exodus to be a sequel to Genesis. About 1877 BC the family of Jacob descended into Egypt. Because of Joseph's position in that land, the Israelites were treated cordially. Eventually a Pharaoh arose who did not know Joseph

(Exodus 1:8). The Israelites were gradually persecuted and then enslaved. Altogether the Israelites were in Egypt 430 years (Exodus 12:40). Toward the end of that period, God raised up a deliverer for his people. That deliverer's name was Moses.

The text does not identify the Pharaoh in Exodus. There is some dispute about Egyptian chronology. If the standard chronology is followed, the Pharaohs mentioned in Exodus belonged to the Eighteenth Dynasty. The Pharaoh who did not know Joseph (Exodus 1:8) may have been one of the Hyksos rulers who invaded Egypt about 1730 BC.

The Pharaoh who launched the intense persecution of the Israelites may have been Ahmoses I. The Pharaoh at the time of the Exodus probably was Amenhotep II.

Moses and the Pharaohs of the Eighteenth Dynasty				
Thutmose I	Thutmose II	Hatshepsut	Thutmose III	Amenhotep II
Moses born 1527 BC	Moses groomed for the throne of Egypt		Moses flees to Midian 1488 BC	Moses returns 1448 BC

Besides Moses, Aaron (Moses' brother and spokesman), and Pharaoh, there are five major characters in Exodus. *Miriam* was the sister of Moses, the leader of Israel's women. *Joshua* was Moses' assistant and commander of Israel's army. *Jethro* (Reuel) was priest of Midian and Moses' father-in-law. *Hobab* was Moses' brother-in-law who accompanied Israel from Sinai. *Zipporah* was Moses' "Cushite" wife.

Plan

Exodus can be summed up in the words *plagues and precepts*. The book is organized into three clearly discernable divisions.

❖ **Call out of Egypt** (Exodus 1–19)

❖ **Covenant at Mount Sinai** (Exodus 20–24)

❖ **Construction of the Tabernacle** (Exodus 25–40)

In the first nineteen chapters Moses speaks about the persecution of Israel (chs. 1–6), the plagues against Egypt (chs. 7–12) and the path to Sinai (chs. 13–19). In these chapters God prepares a deliverer, overcomes the Egyptian antagonists, and finally effects the actual deliverance. Israel's exodus from Egypt was one of the most amazing events in world history. In emancipating his people from slavery the God of the Bible was demonstrating his superiority to the gods of the greatest nation on the face of the earth. God's awesome power met the needs of his desperate people.

The middle chapters of Exodus focus on Israel's consecration at Mount Sinai. This section contains commands, judgments, and ordinances that were designed to set Israel apart from the world of nations as a holy people. *Commands* have to do with moral life (chs. 19–20), *judgments* with social life (chs. 21–23) and *ordinances* with religious life (chs. 24–40). God organized his people into a nation with the Ten Commandments as their constitution. These chapters reveal the holiness of God and the obligations of the people who served him.

The last sixteen chapters of Exodus focus for the most part on the construction of a tent-shrine. God promised his people that this tent was to be the place where he dwelled in the midst of his people. The Tabernacle was first verbally designed in detail by God (chs. 25–31). The actual construction was delayed by the sin of the people at the foot of the mountain (chs. 32–34). Because of the intercession by Moses the Lord finally authorized the construction of the shrine in chapters 35–40. The structure of the Tabernacle underscored the holiness of God. At the same time, it portrayed his eagerness to fellowship with people.

As for chronology, Exodus briefly summarizes how Israel came into Egypt and became enslaved. The book then focuses on about two years. The plagues lasted about nine months. After leaving Egypt the Israelites spent over eleven months traveling to Mount Sinai and camping there (Exodus 40:2, 17). The two years upon which Exodus focuses are 1448–1447 BC.

Geographically, Exodus also displays a three-stage format: Israel in Egypt and Moses in Sinai (chs. 1–12); Israel en route to Mount Sinai (chs. 13–19); and Israel at Mount Sinai (chs. 20–40).

Eternal Purpose

Obviously Exodus was written in order to continue the history of the Israelite people in the earliest days of their nationhood. The deeper purpose of the book is to reveal through law, ritual, and symbol the character of God.

There are four basic themes in Exodus. The first theme is *redemption*, portrayed in the Passover. The second theme is *deliverance*, portrayed in the exodus from Egypt. The third theme is *governance*, as set forth in the law revealed at Mount Sinai. The fourth theme is *worship*, as set forth in the Tabernacle chapters.

Redemption. As the Lord directed, each Israelite family smeared the blood of a lamb on the doorposts of their residence. As the death angel passed through the land of Egypt he passed over the houses where there was blood. The firstborn sons in those houses were spared. They were redeemed from death by the blood of the lamb. This redemption was celebrated in the Passover meal that was rich in symbolism. The Israelites ate unleavened bread and bitter herbs that night. They ate with their robes girded up about their waists and their staves in their hands (Exodus 12).

Deliverance. God blasted Egypt with ten plagues in order to bring about Israel's deliverance from bondage. The plagues gradually intensified. A pattern is discernible in the first nine plagues. In each set of three plagues the first two were announced by Moses in advance, the last one was unannounced. The first three plagues affected the entire land of Egypt. The next six were experienced only by the Egyptians. The final plague was a special case.

Plagues Against Egypt			
First Triad	**Second Triad**	**Third Triad**	**Last Plague**
1. Water to blood 2. Frogs 3. Lice (gnats)	4. Flies 5. Cattle disease 6. Boils	7. Hail 8. Locusts 9. Darkness	10. Death of the Firstborn
Whole Land Affected	Only Egypt Affected		Protected by Blood

Governance. At Mount Sinai God gave to Israel the law by which the nation was to be governed. God's law defined a just, moral way of life for Old Testament Israel. Its concern for the poor and oppressed, its concepts of a criminal justice system, its ecological concern for the land, and its emphasis on equality for all were centuries ahead of their time. The Ten Commandments are a summary of all that God expected of his people. The first four of these laws describe man's duty to God; the last six define man's relationship to his fellow man.

Ten Commandments	
Duty to God	**Duty to Man**
1. No other gods. 2. No graven images. 3. No profanity. 4. Remember the Sabbath.	5. Honor father and mother. 6. Do not murder. 7. Do not commit adultery. 8. Do not steal. 9. Do not lie. 10. Do not covet
Summarized	**Summarized**
Love the LORD your God *with all your heart* *(Matt 22:37)*	*Love your neighbor* *as yourself* *(Matt 22:39)*

Worship. Exodus is also concerned about worship. This book reports the origins of most of the religious ceremonies and customs of Israel, the construction of the Tabernacle, and the formation of the priesthood and sacrificial system. As such, Exodus is foundational for the following history of Israel. Under God's directions Moses introduced a unique design for worship. It underscored the holiness of God and the sinfulness of mankind. It provided access to God for penitent sinners. The worship system introduced in Exodus sets forth basic principles that are still applicable in the Christian Age.

Anticipation

There are no direct predictions of the coming of Messiah in Exodus. There are, however, a number of types or previews of the Christian Age. Aaron the high priest is a type of Christ who is our high priest (Hebrews 5:4-5). The lawgiver Moses is a type of Christ as our great prophet and teacher (John 1:17). Egypt, the land of Israel's bondage, is a type of the bondage of sin. The Red Sea is a type of baptism (1 Corinthians 10:2).

The Passover lamb of Exodus 12 is a type of Christ who died so that we might not experience God's wrath (1 Corinthians 5:7). The manna provided by God during the wilderness journey is a type of Christ or Christ's words (John 6:58). The rock from which water came forth is a type of the water of life that Christ provides to his followers (1 Corinthians 10:24).

The grand type of Exodus is the Tabernacle. The sacred shrine was designed to set forth the spiritual realities of the Christian Age. The outer court is the world. The holy place within the tent is a type of the church. The holy of holies where the ark was kept is a type of heaven (Hebrews 9:12). The typology of the Tabernacle furniture is set forth in the following chart.

Typology of the Tabernacle Furniture		
Furniture	Symbolical Meaning to Israelites	Typical Meaning to Christians
Bronze Altar	Atonement through Sacrifice	Christ our altar (Heb 13:10)
Bronze Laver	Cleansing from Defilement	Baptism (Titus 3:5)
Table of Showbread	Spiritual Sustenance	Christ the Bread of Life (John 6:35); the Lord's Supper
Lampstand	Illumination through Revelation	Christ is Light of the world (John 8:12); Christians reflect this light.
Incense Altar	Acceptable Supplication	Prayer in the name of Jesus (Rev 8:3-4)
Ark of the Covenant	Access through Covenant Relationship	Christ embodies a New Covenant (1 Cor 11:25)

Keys

Without question the key chapters in the Book of Exodus are chapters 12–14. These chapters record Israel's deliverance from Egyptian bondage.

The key verses in the book are probably these: *You yourselves have seen what I did to Egypt, and how I carried you on eagles' wings and brought you to myself. ⁵Now if you obey me fully and keep my covenant, then out of all nations you will be my treasured possession. Although the whole earth is mine, ⁶you will be for me a kingdom of priests and a holy nation* (Exodus 19:4-6a). Other possibilities for key verses are 3:8 or 12:51.

The key phrase in Exodus is this: *as the LORD commanded Moses* (15 times). The key words in Exodus are *deliver* or *delivered*, which are used thirteen times.

Special Features

Five facts related to Exodus are worthy of note:

- ❖ The ten plagues seem to have been aimed specifically at individual Egyptian gods.
- ❖ The *Red Sea* of Exodus is more properly translated *Sea of Reeds*. This does not mean, however, that the Israelites crossed some marsh. *Sea of Reeds* was the ancient name for the Red Sea. The Greek version and two New Testament passages verify that Israel actually crossed the Red Sea (Acts 7:36; Hebrews 11:29).
- ❖ There are two kinds of laws in Exodus. An *apodictic* law is worded like this: *Do not do such and such.* A casuistic law is worded: *If a man does X, then his punishment will be Y.*
- ❖ The modern state of Israel captured the Sinai Peninsula from Egypt in the Six-Day War of 1967. This is the same area where the ancient Israelites wandered for forty years. The Israelis returned the Sinai Peninsula to Egypt as a result of the Egyptian-Israeli peace treaty in 1979.
- ❖ On the Mount of Transfiguration, Moses and Elijah spoke with Jesus about his *decease* (KJV), lit., his *exodus* (Luke 9:31).

HEAR

God has spoken in Exodus. We should be willing to hear. You can sample the book by studying the following outstanding chapters:

- ❖ Baby Moses in the river reeds (Exodus 1)
- ❖ Moses' call to service (Exodus 3–4)
- ❖ Ten plagues and a battle of wills (Exodus 7–11)
- ❖ Passover instituted (Exodus 12)
- ❖ Crossing the Red Sea (Exodus 14)
- ❖ Tablets with Ten Commandments (Exodus 20)
- ❖ Glory fills the Tabernacle (Exodus 40)

Here are some of the favorite lines in Exodus:

- ❖ *I AM* (Exodus 3:14): God's name as revealed to Moses.
- ❖ *"Let my people go"* (Exodus 5:1): Moses' demand to Pharaoh.
- ❖ *You shall have no other gods before me* (Exodus 20:3): the first Commandment.
- ❖ *Life for life, eye for an eye, tooth for tooth* (Exodus 21:23-24). The punishment must fit the crime.
- ❖ *"Whoever is for the LORD? come to me"* (Exodus 32:26).
- ❖ *The LORD, the LORD, the compassionate and gracious God, slow to anger, abounding in love and faithfulness* (Exodus 34:6).

CHAPTER THREE

FOUNDATION BOOKS (2)

Leviticus–Deuteronomy

n the previous chapter we surveyed the first two of the Foundation Books. In this chapter we will get acquainted with the next three books on this shelf. The Book of Exodus concluded with the dedication of the Tabernacle. The Book of Leviticus will show us how that Tabernacle was used. The Book of Numbers relates the journeys of the Israelites from Mount Sinai to the edge of the Promised Land. The Book of Deuteronomy records Moses' last words to Israel before his death.

3rd Bible Book
Book of Leviticus
Sacrifice and Sanctity

As with the two previous books, Jewish tradition refers to the third book of the Bible by the first Hebrew word, *Vayyiqra* = *and he called.* Leviticus (*Leh-viht'-ih-kuhs* means *pertaining to Levites.* This name goes back to the Latin and Greek Bibles.

The book contains twenty-seven chapters organized into 859 verses. Leviticus contains 24,546 words.

Situation

The human author of Leviticus is Moses. Fifty-six times this book claims that God gave laws to his people through Moses.

New Testament citations confirm the claims of the book (Matthew 8:4; Luke 2:22; Hebrews 8:5). Leviticus was written about 1444 BC during Israel's forty-year wilderness wandering.

Clearly Leviticus was intended to be the sequel to Exodus. In Exodus God gets his people out of Egypt; in Leviticus he tries to get Egypt out of his people. The former book begins with enslaved sinners; Leviticus begins with redeemed saints. Exodus shows the way out of bondage; Leviticus reveals the way into God's presence. Deliverance is the theme of Exodus; dedication is the theme of Leviticus. In Exodus God speaks from the top of a mountain; in Leviticus, from the tent of meeting. In Exodus God told his people how to build the Tabernacle; in Leviticus he shows them how to utilize that structure. In Exodus there is redemption and instruction for God's people; in Leviticus God's people grow in fellowship, holiness, and worship.

In Genesis God announced that the remedy for man's sin was a future descendant of woman, the Messiah. In Exodus God answered man's cry for deliverance by providing the blood of the Passover lamb. Now in Leviticus God makes a twofold provision for man's need, namely sacrifice and priesthood.

Plan

The Book of Leviticus can be summed up in the words *sacrifices and sanctity*. The book consists mostly of legislative material. It contains civil law, ceremonial law, moral law, religious law, and sanitary law. Everything in the book, however, is calculated to stimulate spiritual life. For example, the sanitary and dietary laws are not laid down primarily for health reasons, but as distinctive marks of a chosen people. The detailed rituals that are prescribed express the sense of the holiness of God in whose service the rituals were to be exercised. The effect of these laws was to make Israel a holy nation.

Only two historical narratives are found within this legal book. First, Moses speaks in detail about the consecration of the priests and death of Aaron's two sons (Leviticus 8–10). Second, Moses relates the story of how Israel executed a blasphemer, the son of a certain Shelomith (Leviticus 24:10-14).

Moses has organized his third book in two major divisions. The first depicts the *way to God* or attaining fellowship with a holy God (chs. 1–16). The second major division outlines the *walk with God* or maintaining fellowship with the Lord (chs. 17–27).

The first sixteen chapters focus on how to approach God under the Mosaic system. In these chapters Moses presents offering laws (chs. 1–7), priestly laws (chs. 8–10), and purity laws (chs. 11–15). The first main division culminates in the annual ritual for the Day of Atonement (ch. 16) in which the sinfulness of the nation was rolled forward another year until the final Day of Atonement when Jesus died on the cross.

The last eleven chapters of Leviticus set forth how the Israelites are to live as a holy people. The emphasis in this section is on holy people (chs. 17–22), holy times (chs. 23–25), and holy vows (chs. 26–27), in other words sanctification, celebration, and obligation. The structure of the book reverses the thought content of Leviticus 19:2, *Be holy because I, the* LORD *your God, am holy*. From a New Testament perspective the book reflects the same twofold emphasis of 1 John 1:7 (*The blood purifies us . . . if we walk in the light*).

Chronologically Leviticus covers only about a month of Israel's stay at Mount Sinai. The last event in Exodus is the erection of the Tabernacle on New Year's day of the second year of Israel's departure from Egypt (Exodus 40:2). The first event in the Book of Numbers — a military census — took place one month later (Numbers 1:1). All the legislation in Leviticus must have been given during the intervening month.

Biographically the leading figures in Leviticus are Moses and Aaron. In a subordinate role are the four sons of Aaron (Nadab, Abihu, Eleazar, Ithamar).

Eternal Purpose

The purpose of Leviticus is to show Old Testament Israel how to live as a priestly kingdom and holy nation. The ultimate purpose of the book is to underscore the thought that God is holy and that he requires his people to be holy. In reading this book it is easy to get bogged down in all the details of God's Law. One may miss the main point if he spends too much time trying to analyze why God orders the Israelites to perform all these rituals and obey these rules—some of which may seem bizarre and even unfair. Instead, the book should be read as a picture book illustrating fundamental principles of salvation: the seriousness of sin and the importance of obeying God.

Since God is the same yesterday, today, and forever, Leviticus is a window to the divine character. The book sets forth in symbols the basic principles that underlie all dealings between God and men. At the same time, Leviticus sheds light on principles that should govern society.

Years ago Griffith-Thomas[1] suggested that the teaching of Leviticus revolves around seven great truths. Slightly modified these great truths are the following: The great *problem* of mankind is sin. The great *provision* for man's redemption is sacrifice. The great *prerequisite* for approaching God is priesthood. The great *plan* is the annual Day of Atonement. The great *possibility* is access to God. The great *principle* underlying all of God's actions and requirements is holiness. The great *privilege* of redeemed people is to stand in the presence of God.

The old saying cleanliness is next to godliness is not in the Bible; but the teaching of Leviticus comes close to making that affirmation. Leviticus speaks about clean food (ch. 11), clean bodies (12:1–13:46), clean clothes (13:47-59), clean houses (14:33-57), clean contacts (ch. 15), and a clean nation (ch. 16). Through broad principle and specific precept God governed every aspect of the life of his people Israel. The demands of this book may be summed up in the words of the Apostle Paul: *whether you eat or drink or whatever you do, do it all for the glory of God* (1 Corinthians 10:31).

Anticipation

Leviticus contains no messianic prophecies. The book, however, is a treasury of types—previews of the spiritual realities of the new covenant age. Here is the New Testament gospel for sin-

---

[1] W.H. Griffith-Thomas, *Through the Pentateuch Chapter by Chapter* (Grand Rapids: Kregel, 1985) 110.

ners stated in Old Testament language and enshrined in the ritual of sacrifice. The Old Testament offerings, appointed times, priestly consecration, and office of high priest were all designed by God to portray the spiritual realities of the Christian Age.

Mosaic offerings. God prescribed five basic sacrifices for ancient Israel. Each of these offerings depicted a specific aspect of the great sacrifice of Christ on the cross. In the **burnt offering** (Leviticus 6:8-13) the carcass of the animal (minus the hide) was totally burned on the altar. This offering symbolized the worshiper's total commitment to God. As a type the burnt offering portrays the perfect commitment of Christ. Using language associated with the burnt offering, Paul says that Christ's offering was an aroma pleasing before the Lord (Ephesians 5:2). As Christians we offer our lives as a consecrated sacrifice to the Lord (Romans 12:1-2).

In the **meal offering** the Israelite offered grain or unleavened cakes as a symbol of the consecration of possessions to God (Leviticus 6:14-23). Leaven or yeast symbolized corruption, and the lack thereof, purity. So as a type the meal offering points to the perfect manhood of Christ. His sinless life made Christ's sacrifice acceptable before God. Under Old Testament law the priests were required to consume the cakes of the meal offering. So Christians, as the present-day priests of God, must feed daily on Christ, the bread of life (John 6:35).

In the peace or **fellowship offering** (Leviticus 7:11-36) a portion of the sacrificial animal was offered up to God. The rest of the animal was cooked and eaten by the worshipers in a fellowship meal. For the Israelites this offering symbolized communion between God and his people. As a type the peace offering points to Christ who is our peace (Ephesians 2:14). Because of his sacrifice on the cross we have peace with God (Romans 5:1).

In the **sin offering** (Leviticus 4:1–5:13) the blood of the sacrificial animal was smeared on the horns (protrusions) of the altar. The carcass was then burned outside the camp. The symbolism of this offering is that sin is covered by blood, removed, and judged.

The sin offering points to the fact that Christ is our sin offering (2 Corinthians 5:21; 1 Peter 2:24; Galatians 1:4; Hebrews 13:12). Our sins have been covered by Christ's blood.

The **trespass offering** (Leviticus 5:14–6:11; 7:1-6) required restitution for something that was wrongfully taken plus a penalty. From this offering the Israelites learned that sin demands payment of a price. As a type the trespass offering points to the fact that Christ gave his life as a ransom for our sins (Matthew 20:28). Our sin debt was paid in full by Christ's death on the cross.

Appointed times. There are eleven appointed times under the Mosaic system. At least nine of them are types pointing forward to the spiritual realities of the Christian Age. The seventh day of each week was a **Sabbath** (Leviticus 23:3; Exodus 20:8-11; Deuteronomy 5:12-15). This day of rest celebrated God's rest during creation week and Israel's release from Egyptian bondage. As a type the Sabbath points forward to the eternal Sabbath rest of God's people (Hebrews 4:1-6).

The **new moon** festival was celebrated either every month or quarterly (Numbers 28:11-15; 10:10; Ezekiel 46:1-3). On this day there were special sacrifices at the Tabernacle, rest by the people, and the blowing of trumpets. No typological significance of this appointed time is suggested in the New Testament.

The **Passover** feast (Leviticus 23:5; Numbers 28:16; Deuteronomy 16:1-2) was celebrated annually during the spring of the year. This feast commemorated Israel's redemption from Egyptian bondage. A lamb was eaten by each family along with bitter herbs and unleavened bread. Paul declared that Christ is the Christian's Passover (1 Corinthians 5:7). It is he who delivered us from the bondage of sin.

For seven days after Passover the feast of **unleavened bread** was observed by Israel (Exodus 23:15; Leviticus 23:6-8; Numbers 28:17-25; Deuteronomy 16:3-8). This feast commemorated how Israel left Egypt in haste. Unleavened bread was eaten throughout the week of the feast. The feast of unleavened bread points to the holy walk of believers (1 Corinthians 5:8).

The ceremony of **first fruits** (Leviticus 23:9-14; Exodus 23:16; Numbers 28:26-31) was conducted on the first Sabbath following Passover. This was the beginning of the barley harvest. A sheaf of grain was offered at the Tabernacle. This ceremony pointed forward to the resurrection of Christ (1 Corinthians 15:33).

The **feast of weeks** or Pentecost (Leviticus 23:15-22; Exodus 34:22; Numbers 28:26; Deuteronomy 16:9-12) came seven weeks plus a day after Passover Sabbath. This festival commemorated the law being given at Sinai and the completion of the barley harvest. Two loaves of bread were brought to the Tabernacle and special sacrifices were offered. This festival points forward to the coming of the Holy Spirit and beginning of the church (Acts 2:4).

The **feast of trumpets** (Leviticus 23:23-25; Numbers 29:1-6) on the first day of the seventh month heralded the beginning of the religious new year. Blowing of trumpets and special sacrifices marked this day. The feast of trumpets was a type of the gathering of God's people (Matthew 24:31).

The **Day of Atonement** (Leviticus 23:26-32; ch. 16; Numbers 29:7-11) was observed on the tenth day of the seventh month. This day commemorated the covering and removal of Israel's sin for another year. A bull and goat were sacrificed. Blood was sprinkled on the mercy seat of the ark within the holy of holies. Sins were confessed over another goat which then was driven into the wilderness. The Mosaic Day of Atonement pointed forward to the atoning work of Christ upon the cross.

The **feast of Tabernacles** or **ingathering** was also celebrated in the seventh month. For seven days the Israelites lived in crude booths or huts to commemorate the time when Israel resided in the wilderness for forty years. This joyous festival pointed forward to the worship in the days of Messiah (Zechariah 14:16-18).

The **sabbatical year** was observed every seventh year in Israel (Leviticus 25:1-7; Exodus 23:11-12; Deuteronomy 15:2-18). During the entire year the land was left untilled to recognize that God was the owner of all the land. There is no typological significance to this appointed time in the New Testament.

Every fiftieth year was called a **Jubilee** in Israel (Leviticus 25:8-55). The beginning of the Jubilee was marked by the blowing of a ram's horn. During the Jubilee property reverted to the original owner, debt was remitted, and slaves were released. This appointed time was a type of the Gospel Age (Isaiah 61:2; Luke 4:19).

Priestly consecration. The Mosaic priesthood (Leviticus 5) is a type or preview of the New Testament priesthood of all believers in Christ. A number of comparisons can be made between the two priesthoods. Like the Old Testament priesthood we are called to this ministry (Exodus 29:4; 1 Peter 2:9). In the consecration service the Mosaic priests were washed in water, and so were we (Acts 22:16; Hebrews 10:22; Titus 3:5). The Mosaic priests were robed in holy garments, and so were we (Galatians 3:27; Revelation 3:18; Romans 13:14). Old Testament priests were anointed with oil, symbolic of the Holy Spirit. Christians have received the anointing of the Holy Spirit (1 John 2:20, 27; 4:13; Acts 2:38). The Mosaic priests had blood sprinkled upon their garments. Christian priests wear robes washed in the blood of Christ (Revelation 7:14). Old Testament priests had their bodies sprinkled with blood, as do Christian priests (Hebrews 10:22). Mosaic priests were made holy (Exodus 29:21), as are Christian priests (Hebrews 10:10). Old Testament priests were permitted to partake of the sin offering. We partake of Christ who is our sin offering (Hebrews 13:10-12).

High priesthood. Under the Mosaic system Aaron, Moses' older brother, was designated by God to be the first high priest of Israel (Leviticus 16). As high priest, Aaron is a type of Christ our high priest. Aaron was called of God from among men, as was Christ (Hebrews 5:4, 10). The Old Testament high priest had compassion for the wayward (Hebrews 5:2), as does Christ (Hebrews 5:7). The high priest functioned in spotless purity of dress, a type of the spotless purity of Christ's character. On the Day of Atonement the high priest entered the holy of holies whereas at his ascension Christ entered heaven itself, the ultimate holy of holies (Hebrews 9:24). In the holy of holies Aaron secured atonement for Israel by offering the blood of a goat. Christ made complete atonement by offering his own blood. Aaron offered the blood for the entire nation of Israel including himself. Christ offered himself as a sacrifice for the whole human race (John 3:16), but not for himself. The Old Testament high priest offered sacrifice in the holy of holies continually from year to year; but Christ offered himself once for all eternity (Hebrews 9:25).

Keys

Leviticus 16, which records the ritual for the Day of Atonement, must be considered the key chapter in the book.

Without question the key verse is Leviticus 19:2, *Be holy because I, the* LORD *your God, am holy.* As noted above, this verse virtually outlines the contents of Leviticus in reverse order.

The key phrase in Leviticus is *before the* LORD, which occurs about sixty times.

Key words in Leviticus are *holy* and cognates—about 131 times; *clean* with cognates and contrasts—about 186 times; *offering* or *sacrifice*—over ninety times; and *blood*—88 times.

Special Features

Three facts related to Leviticus stand out:

❖ The Liberty Bell in Philadelphia is inscribed with words taken from Leviticus that were part of the year of Jubilee ritual: *proclaim liberty throughout the land* (Leviticus 25:10).

❖ The idea of a *scapegoat* as one who takes the blame for something someone else did is taken from the KJV of Leviticus 16.

❖ Nearly all of Leviticus is in the form of speeches of God.

HEAR

There are several reasons why most Christians never read Leviticus. Some think it is impossible for them to master all the ritual and symbol in this book. Others suppose that since the Levitical laws have now long passed away, they have no relevance to the modern world. Still others avoid the book because they perceive that some of the Levitical requirements, in their severity or apparent triviality, are at variance with what we know of God from other Scripture.

It is true that as ceremonial requirements, the laws of Leviticus are no longer valid. Their underlying principles, however, are as valid today as during the days of Moses.

Leviticus is not easy reading. Nonetheless, God SPEAKS in this book, and we must HEAR what he has to say. This book requires your concentration. To get a taste of Leviticus start with these outstanding chapters:

❖ The first priests begin their ministry (Leviticus 9)
❖ Two priests offer strange fire (Leviticus 10)
❖ Day of Atonement ritual (Leviticus 16)

There are not many verses in Leviticus that will make anyone's list of favorite Bible memory verses. One literature teacher remarked: "Leviticus is a dust heap containing a single pearl— Leviticus 19:18b (*Love your neighbor as yourself*)." Aside from this gem and the key verse in the book (19:2) only one other verse might be listed as a famous line from Leviticus: *I will walk among you and be your God, and you will be my people* (Leviticus 26:12).

4th Bible Book

Book of Numbers
Marching and Murmuring

Jews refer to the fourth book of the Bible by the first word of the Hebrew text, *Bemidhbar* = *in the wilderness*. The name *Numbers* comes from the Greek and Latin Bibles. The name is derived from the fact that two national censuses are recorded in this book.

With thirty-six chapters, 1,288 verses, and 32,902 words Numbers is the fifth largest book in the Old Testament.

The Book of Numbers is intimately connected to the previous books. In Genesis God chose a people, in Exodus he redeemed them, in Leviticus he sanctified them, and in Numbers he disciplined them. Numbers takes up the story where Leviticus left off, at Mount Sinai. In Leviticus we see the believer's worship and purity; in Numbers the believer's walk and pilgrimage. Numbers illustrates Romans 11:22 (*Consider therefore the kindness and sternness of God*).

Situation

Numbers is about transition. *Marching and murmuring* characterizes the narratives of this book. After being liberated from Egypt the Israelites traveled to Mount Sinai. There they received God's law (Exodus–Leviticus). This was their past. Israel's future was to be in the land God promised to give Abraham's descendants (Genesis). Numbers tells the story of the journey from Sinai to Canaan, the last stage of the long trail that led from slavery to rest in the Promised Land.

The Book of Numbers was written by Moses, at the end of Israel's wilderness wandering and just before his death. The year was about 1407 BC. The narrative of the journey from Sinai to the plains of Moab is attributed to Moses. The book also claims that the regulations and laws contained therein were given through the agency of Moses (e.g., Numbers 1:1).

It took Israel a month and a half to make the trip from Egypt to Sinai (Exodus 19:1). During the next ten months the Israelites received instructions from the Lord and constructed the Tabernacle. The priesthood was consecrated to the service of God. The command to take the first census came twelve and a half months after the Israelites left Egypt, or after they had encamped at Sinai for eleven months (Numbers 1:1).

Plan

The Book of Numbers contains lists, census tallies, and laws as well as historical narrative. Moses is interpreter of the history of his people. In every event he sees the guiding hand of God. The Most High watches over his people. He provides for their wants. He keeps his covenant with them. God prepares them by means of a severe discipline for being his witness to the world.

Chronological plan. Numbers covers about thirty-nine years. The opening scene in the book is a military census at Mount Sinai one month after the Tabernacle had been set up (Exodus 40:1; Numbers 1:1). The Israelites departed from Mount Sinai nineteen days after the Tabernacle was erected (Numbers 10:11). About eleven months later they arrived at Kadesh (Numbers 20:1). The last dated event in the book is the death of Aaron thirty-seven years and four months after arriving at Kadesh (Numbers 33:38). We should probably allow four or five additional months for the remaining events in Numbers.

Biographical plan. The leading figure in Numbers is again Moses. The narrative is built around four crises in which others interacted with Moses. The first crisis was a rebellion against Moses by **Aaron** and **Miriam**, Moses' brother and sister (Numbers 12).

The second crisis came at Kadesh when the nation listened to the negative report of ten spies. The Israelites lost faith in the power of God to give to them the Promised Land. They turned against Moses. In this crisis **Joshua** and **Caleb** stand out as two spies who believed Israel could conquer Canaan (Numbers 13–14).

Crisis three also took place at Kadesh. **Korah, Dathan,** and **Abiram** led a rebellion against the civil leadership of Moses and the priestly leadership of Aaron (Numbers 16).

The fourth crisis took place as Israel was camped in the plains of Moab. The Moabite king **Balak** tried to subvert Israel by enlisting the aid of a greedy prophet named **Balaam**. God did not permit Balaam to utter a curse against Israel. Then King Balak resorted to more earthy subversion. He used the women of his land to lure the men of Israel into idolatry. Zimri (an Israelite chief) and Cozbi (a Midianite princess) were slain by **Phinehas** while committing adultery within the camp of Israel (Numbers 25).

Others who are worthy of mention in Numbers are these: **Eleazar** who succeeded his father Aaron as high priest; **Sihon** and **Og,** two kings defeated by Israel. **Eldad** and **Medad** who prophesied even though they did not go up to the Tabernacle as directed by Moses.

Geographical plan. The events in Numbers transpire in six venues. The book opens at Mount Sinai (Numbers 1:1–10:10) where a census was taken and additional laws were set forth.

The second venue was the desert between Sinai and Kadesh (Numbers 10:11–12:16). Normally the trip from Sinai to Kadesh took only eleven days (Deuteronomy 1:2). Israel, however, moved only at the direction of God. Therefore it took Israel about ten months and ten days to make the trip. En route they stopped to camp twenty-one times (Numbers 33:16-36).

The third venue was Kadesh (Numbers 13:1–20:21). Kadesh seems to have served as a hub for the activities of Israel for most of thirty-eight years.

The fourth venue is the rugged territory between Kadesh and the Arnon Gorge (Numbers 20:22–21:15).

The fifth venue is the region of Transjordan (the area east of the Jordan River). This area was occupied at the time by two Amorite kings, Sihon and Og. Both kings were defeated by Israel. Their land was designated for occupation by two and a half tribes of Israel (Numbers 21:21-35).

The final scenes in Numbers play out in the Plains of Moab (Numbers 22:1–36:13).

Eternal Purpose

The purpose of Numbers is to relate the history of God's people from the time of the first census at Sinai until the encampment in the plains of Moab. The greater purpose of the book is to stress the lesson that perseverance in the work of God is essential.

The Book of Numbers teaches many valuable lessons. Freedom needs law such as one finds in Exodus–Leviticus; it also needs discipline such as is revealed in Numbers. The book demonstrates that God gave ample physical and spiritual provision for his people en route to Canaan. God's forbearance is indicated in the fact that he did not abandon his people even when they rebelled against him time and again.

Numbers aims to underscore the consequence of disbelief and disobedience to God. The book relates how the Lord disciplined his people but remained faithful to his covenant promises in spite of their fickleness. Numbers displays the patience, holiness, justice, and mercy of God toward his people.

The abiding lesson of the book is that God uses trials and tests to help his people grow in commitment. While it may be necessary for us to pass through wilderness experiences, we do not have to camp out there. For Israel, an eleven-day journey became a forty-year ordeal because of disobedience and disbelief.

Two extensive New Testament passages turn to Israel's wilderness experience for illustrations of spiritual truth. In 1 Corinthians 10:1-12 events in Numbers illustrate the danger of self-indulgence and immorality. In Hebrews 3:7–4:6 they illustrate the theme of entering God's rest through faith.

Anticipation

In Numbers there is one direct prediction of the coming of Messiah. It is found in Balaam's fourth oracle (Numbers 24:17-19). God enabled Balaam to foresee the rise of a mighty King within Israel, one who will vanquish all the enemies of God's people. The context indicates that this Ruler was to arise after the Greek conquerors of the Near East were themselves conquered by others (24:24). In other words, God revealed through Balaam that the Messiah was to appear during the Roman period.

There are in Numbers three major types or previews of Christian Age realities. First, Aaron's rod that budded (Numbers 17) is a type of the resurrection of Jesus.

Second, the ashes of a red heifer (Numbers 19) + cedar wood + hyssop + scarlet thread were burned. Water was poured through the ashes to produce special water for cleansing. This ritual was a picture of Christ's cleansing believers from the acts that lead to death (Hebrews 9:14) or works produced prior to being made alive in Christ.

Third, the bronze serpent that brought healing to snakebitten people in the camp of Israel (Numbers 21) depicts Christ dying on the cross for the salvation of mankind (John 3:14-16).

Keys

The key chapter in the Book of Numbers is chapter 14. This chapter records Israel's failure of faith at Kadesh, and the consequent sentence to wander forty years in the wilderness.

The key verses in the book are these: *In this desert your bodies will fall — every one of you twenty years old or more who was counted in the census and who has grumbled against me. ³⁰Not one of you will enter the land . . . except Caleb . . . and Joshua* (Numbers 14:29-30).

The key phrase in Numbers is *all that were able to go forth to war* (14 times).

The key words in the books are *service* (45); *war* (31); and *wilderness* (45).

Special Features

Here are a few facts that relate to the Book of Numbers.

❖ Some think that the star of David — the national symbol of the modern state of Israel — comes from Balaam's prophecy that a future king will appear like a star (Numbers 24:17).

❖ Balaam's prophecy (Numbers 24) may have triggered the search of the magi when they saw a new star in the east (Matthew 2:2).

❖ The name of Balaam (Numbers 22:4-5) has shown up on a seventh-century BC plaster inscription found among ancient non-Israelite ruins in Jordan. The words describe Balaam as a "seer of the gods" who received a divine message about a coming disaster.

❖ The count of over 600,000 fighting men in Israel suggests that the entire group that traveled through the desert was over two million.

❖ The medical symbol of two snakes on a staff (called *caduceus*) has nothing to do with the biblical incident in which Moses erected a bronze serpent on a pole. The caduceus was the symbol of Aesculapius, the Roman god of healing.

HEAR

Numbers should not be read as merely a historical report of ancient Israel's experience in the wilderness. The Christian can find in this book an analogy of every believer's experience. We too have been redeemed from bondage. We are on a journey to God's Promised Land. Like Israel's journey to Canaan, ours is also filled with tests and challenges. As was the case then, so now only an obedient faith can preserve us from disasters along the way.

Here are some suggestions for a sampling of what this great book has to offer:

- ❖ Twelve spies sent to spy out Canaan (Numbers 13)
- ❖ The people rebel against Moses (Numbers 14)
- ❖ A bronze serpent brings healing to snakebitten people (Numbers 21)
- ❖ Balaam tries to curse Israel (Numbers 22–24)
- ❖ A holy war against Midian (Numbers 31)

Some of the favorite lines in this book are these:

- ❖ *The* LORD *. . . does not leave the guilty unpunished; he punishes the children for the sin of the fathers to the third and fourth generation* (Numbers 14:18).
- ❖ *Make a snake and put it up on a pole; anyone who is bitten can look at it and live* (Numbers 21:8).
- ❖ *Because you did not trust in me enough to honor me as holy in the sight of the Israelites, you will not bring this community into the land I give them* (Numbers 20:12).

5ᵗʰ Bible Book
Book of Deuteronomy
Preaching and Pleading

In the Jewish tradition the fifth book of the Bible is named after the first word in the Hebrew text *Haddebharim* = *the words.* The name *Deuteronomy* (*dew-tur-ron'-oh-mee*) is derived from the Latin and Greek versions of the Old Testament. This name means *second law.*

The book contains thirty-four chapters, 958 verses, and 28,461 words.

Situation

The human author of Deuteronomy was Moses. The time and place of this book are clearly indicated (1:1-5; 3:29; 4:46). There are specific claims within the book that the material comes from Moses (1:1-6; 4:44-46; 29:1; 31:9, 24-26). Furthermore, New Testament citations (over eighty) attribute the book to Moses (e.g., Romans 10:6-8; Hebrews 12:29; 13:5; Matthew 4:4, 7, 10; 22:37-38).

The concluding verses of Deuteronomy report the death of Moses. Obviously Moses did not write these verses. They were probably appended by the writer of the next volume of the sacred collection. Nonetheless, Moses was the primary writer of this book. He probably completed this book shortly before his death in 1407 BC.

In the Book of Numbers Israel arrived at the border of the Promised Land. Deuteronomy prepares them to enter that land. It was necessary for Moses to reiterate the basic precepts of the law, and make a few adjustments in that law, for the following reasons. First, a new generation had arisen. Second, a new land was before them. Third, they were encountering new dangers, e.g., the allurement of Baal worship. Fourth, they had new prospects. They were about to replace homeless wandering with a homeland at last. Fifth, Israel faced new challenges militarily, economically, and spiritually. Sixth, there were new duties to be explained, duties appropriate to agricultural life. Finally, a new leader was about to emerge.

The only date in Deuteronomy is the first day of the eleventh month after Israel left Egypt (Deuteronomy 1:3). The next date in the sacred record is Israel's passage across the Jordan River on the tenth day of the first month of the forty-first year (Joshua 4:19). So the maximum timeframe for the speeches in Deuteronomy is seventy days.

Geographically the setting for Deuteronomy is the Plains of Moab just east of Jericho on the eastern side of the Jordan River.

Moses' speeches, however, review the entire history of the journey from Egypt.

Plan

The contents of Deuteronomy can be summed up in the phrase *preaching and pleading*. The book consists mostly of farewell messages by Moses to the people he had served for forty years. The exact number of addresses is debated. There are at least four.

Throughout the book Moses makes constant appeal to motives and emotions. His purpose was to move and motivate Israel. In Exodus, Leviticus, and Numbers the Lord was speaking *to* Moses or *through* Moses to the people. Here Moses himself addresses the nation.

In addition to the lengthy sermons, Deuteronomy contains a song (Deuteronomy 32), a blessing (Deuteronomy 33), and three brief historical narratives—an introduction to the book (Deuteronomy 1:1-5), the setting aside of cities of refuge (Deuteronomy 4:41-49), and Moses' final ascent to the scene of his death atop Mount Nebo (Deuteronomy 34:1-12).

The structure of the book looks like this:

- ❖ **Synopsis of the journey** (chs. 1–4)
- ❖ **Summary of the law** (chs. 5–26)
- ❖ **Sermon on responsibility** (chs. 27–28)
- ❖ **Sermon on commitment** (chs. 29–30)
- ❖ **Summons of Moses** (chs. 31–34)

Biographically no new characters are introduced in Deuteronomy. However, in his addresses Moses does refer to a number of characters we encountered earlier. Test your knowledge of the four previous books by attempting to identify the following: Sihon, Og, Abraham, Isaac, Jacob, Caleb, Joshua, Esau, Lot, Pharaoh, Aaron, Eleazar, Dathan, Abiram, and Balaam.

Eternal Purpose

The immediate purpose of Deuteronomy is to review the history and law of Israel for the benefit of the new generation that had grown up during the wilderness period. Ultimately the book was intended to teach that obedience to God is essential. The teaching of the book regarding obedience can be summarized like this:

- ❖ Necessity of obedience: God's law
- ❖ Motive for obedience: God's goodness
- ❖ Standard of obedience: God's word
- ❖ Incentive to obedience: God's faithfulness
- ❖ Alternative to obedience: God's wrath

One could summarize the theology of Deuteronomy in three points. First, Yahweh is a unique God (4:35; 6:4; 7:25; 10:17; et al). Second, Israel is a unique people (4:31; 29:13). Third, a unique relationship exists between God and Israel. He is their Father (32:6). Israel must therefore love and not merely fear him (4:10; 5:29; 6:5; 10:12; et al).

Perhaps the greatest single contribution of Deuteronomy is the light it sheds on the nature of God's covenant with Israel. The book reveals that this covenant was not a contract between two parties. God's covenant with Israel was a proclamation of his sovereignty; it was an instrument for binding the chosen people to him in a commitment of absolute allegiance.

Like Leviticus, Deuteronomy contains a good deal of legal detail; but its emphasis is on the laymen rather than the priests. Moses reminds the new generation of the importance of obedience if they are to learn from the sad example of their parents. Deuteronomy is the later and more popular version of God's law. This is the version of the law which has been widely quoted during centuries since its composition. For this reason Deuteronomy is one of the most influential books ever written.

Anticipation

There is one grand messianic announcement in Deuteronomy. God revealed to Moses that someday *a prophet like unto Moses* was to appear (Deuteronomy 18:14-20). That prophet is identified as Jesus (Acts 3:22-23; 7:37).

Two additional types or previews of Christian realities surface in Deuteronomy. The cities of refuge (Deuteronomy 19:1-13) afforded sanctuary for manslaughters. These cities were a type of Christ to whom we have fled for refuge (Hebrews 6:18). The second type in Deuteronomy is the kinsman-redeemer (Deuteronomy 25:1-10) whose responsibility it was to ransom a kinsman who may have sold himself into slavery (Leviticus 25:47-48). The kinsman-redeemer is a picture of the redemptive work of Christ.

Keys

Chapter 27 is the key chapter in Deuteronomy. This chapter contains the formal ratification of the covenant between God and his people.

The key verses: *And now, O Israel, what does the LORD your God ask of you but to fear the LORD your God, to walk in all his ways, to love him, to serve the LORD your God with all your heart and with all your soul, *¹³*and to observe the LORD's commands and decrees that I am giving you today for your own good?* (Deuteronomy 10:12-13). A number of other verses have also been nominated for the honor of key verse. These are: 4:23; 5:29; 6:4; 7:6-11; 8:11; 11:26-28; 28:1; 29:1.

The key phrases in the book are *the land* (over 100 times) and *this day* (70).

The key words in the book are *possess* + cognates (65); *given* (32); *covenant* (27); *remember* (14); *hear* (50); *do/keep/observe* (155); and *love* (21).

Deuteronomy is the book of remembrance. *Beware lest you forget* is a key theme in Deuteronomy. Forgetting what God has done for us is dangerous because it leads to arrogance and disobedience.

Special Features

A number of facts set Deuteronomy apart as distinctive in the sacred collection.

- ❖ Deuteronomy is a covenant renewal document that uses the same format as Near Eastern treaties from the time of Moses.
- ❖ Deuteronomy was perhaps Christ's favorite book. He quoted from it more than any other. There are nearly a

hundred quotes or references to Deuteronomy in the New Testament.

❖ The concept of refuge for the fugitive goes back to Deuteronomy and the appointment of cities of refuge.

❖ The concept of a father/child relationship between God and his people has its origin in this book (Deuteronomy 1:31).

❖ When he was tempted by the devil in the wilderness, Jesus responded three times with citations from the Book of Deuteronomy.

❖ For its oratorical power, Moses' second discourse (chs. 5–26) has been compared to the classic discourses of Demosthenes and Cicero.

❖ Deuteronomy supplements the previous four books. The book occupies a role similar to that of the Gospel of John compared to the first three Gospels. It fills in missing elements. It gives the spiritual significance of the history found in the previous books.

❖ The creed of Judaism which is recited everyday by the devout comes from Deuteronomy 6:4.

HEAR

To sample the fare of Deuteronomy, start with these outstanding chapters:

❖ Observe and teach God's commands (Deuteronomy 6)

❖ How to detect false prophets (Deuteronomy 13)

❖ Listen to God's future prophet (Deuteronomy 18)

❖ Mountains of blessing and cursing (Deuteronomy 27)

Here are some famous lines found in Deuteronomy:

❖ A basic fact: *Hear, O Israel: The* LORD *our God, the* LORD *is one* (Deuteronomy 6:4).

❖ A basic obligation: *Love the* LORD *your God with all your heart and with all your soul and with all your strength* (Deuteronomy 6:5).

❖ A basic truth: *But he brought us out from there to bring us in and give us the land that he promised on oath to our forefathers* (Deuteronomy 6:23).

❖ A basic relationship: *For you are a people holy to the LORD your God. The LORD your God has chosen you out of all the peoples on the face of the earth to be his people, his treasured possession* (Deuteronomy 7:6).

❖ A basic need: *man does not live on bread alone but on every word that comes from the mouth of the LORD* (Deuteronomy 8:3).

❖ A basic choice: *This day I call heaven and earth as witnesses against you that I have set before you life and death, blessings and curses. Now choose life, so that you and your children may live* (Deuteronomy 30:19).

❖ A death scene: *Moses was a hundred and twenty years old when he died, yet his eyes were not weak nor his strength gone* (Deuteronomy 34:7).

CHAPTER FOUR

FRAMEWORK BOOKS (1)
Joshua–Ruth

The second shelf of the biblical library contains twelve books. This group has no special titles. Since these books all relate events in Israel's history they are generally referred to as the *Historical Books*. In Jewish circles the four books Joshua, Judges, Samuel, Kings are designated as the *Former Prophets*. They received this special title for two reasons. First, these books were written by prophets. Second, the four books reflect a prophetic view of Israel's history.

The Historical Books are anonymous. Jewish tradition assigns them to eight leading figures in Israel's history that will be noted as the individual books are introduced. Most of these books cover a period much longer than the lifetime of one man. It may therefore be safely assumed that the information conveyed in each book rests partly on earlier oral tradition and partly on the use of written sources. The bottom line, however, is that the writers were guided by the Holy Spirit in compiling their works. This guarantees that believers have in these books a totally reliable record of how God worked with his people Israel through the centuries.

Bookwise the twelve historical books begin with the Book of Joshua and end with Esther. Eventwise these books begin with the conquest of Canaan by Israel and conclude with the second governorship of Nehemiah (Nehemiah 13). This means that the

Historical Books cover about a thousand years of biblical history, from 1406–432 BC. Characterwise the Historical Books begin with Joshua and conclude with Nehemiah.

The overall theme of the historical books is *preparation for Christ*. Each book in its own way shows how the Lord was shaping events in the interest of his long-range goal to bring his Son into the world.

6ᵗʰ Bible Book
Book of Joshua
Victory of Obedient Faith

The name of the sixth book of the Bible is taken from the leading character and perhaps the author of the book. The name *Joshua* (Hebrew *Yehoshua*) means *Yahweh is salvation.* In the Greek and Latin Bibles the book bears the same name.

The Book of Joshua contains twenty-four chapters, 658 verses, and 18,858 words.

Situation

Jewish tradition ascribes authorship of the sixth biblical book to Joshua the son of Nun. There is no solid reason for rejecting his authorship. Use of the first person plural pronoun (5:1, 6) supports this view. We know that Joshua could write. In fact he did write material that was considered so sacred that it was recorded in the Book of the Law (Joshua 24:26). Furthermore, the material in the book was written prior to the death of Rahab (Joshua 6:25), a contemporary of Joshua.

Three narratives in the book were probably inserted by the writer of the following book in the sacred collection. Almost certainly that is true of the account of Joshua's death (Joshua 24:31). The writer of the Book of Judges probably also inserted the account of Othniel's capture of Kirjath-sepher (Joshua 15:13-17; cf. Judges 1:9-13) and the note about the migration of the Danites (Joshua 19:47; cf. Judges 18:27-29).

After emerging from the wilderness, Israel fought major battles with the Amorite kings Sihon and Og and later with the

Midianites. During these days they were encamped in the Plains of Moab, opposite Jericho. After an appropriate period of mourning for the death of Moses, the Israelites were ready to march into the land of promise under the leadership of Joshua the son of Nun.

The role of the Book of Joshua in the Scriptures can be seen in a comparison with the two previous books. The Book of Numbers relates the failures of Israel — failure to enter into the land (Numbers 14:2-4), failure to overcome Canaanites (Numbers 14:44-45), failure to occupy Canaan (Numbers 14:28-34). In Joshua these failures are reversed.

In Deuteronomy Moses held forth the prospects of Canaan; he challenged Israel with the *vision* of faith. In Joshua Israel undertakes the *venture* of faith and comes into possession of Canaan. Joshua is the culmination of the promises made to the Patriarchs. At the same time this book is the commencement of a new chapter in the history of God's people.

The Book of Joshua was written about 1380 BC at the conclusion of the conquest of the land just prior to Joshua's death.

Plan

In addition to historical narrative the Book of Joshua contains divine revelations, farewell speeches (chs. 23–24), place lists (chs. 12–21), and prayers. The book is organized in three main divisions:

- ❖ **Entering the Land** (chs. 1–5)
- ❖ **Conquering the Land** (chs. 6–12)
- ❖ **Occupying the Land** (chs. 13–24)

The first major division subdivides into three units: preparation for crossing Jordan (chs. 1–2), passage over Jordan (chs. 3–4), and plan for attacking Jericho (ch. 5).

The second major division describes the three phases in which Israel overcame the Canaanites in the land: central campaign (chs. 6–9), southern campaign (chs. 10), and the northern campaign (chs. 11–12).

The final major division of the book also has three subdivisions: distribution of the land (chs. 13–21), dispute between the tribes (ch. 22), and discourses by Joshua (chs. 23–24).

The author cleverly has indicated the outline of his book in the opening verses of chapter 1.

1:2	*Get ready to cross the Jordan*	(chs. 1–4)
1:5	*No one will be able to stand up against you*	(chs. 5–12)
1:6	*Be strong and courageous*	(chs. 13–22)
1:7	*Obey all the law my servant Moses gave you*	(chs. 23–24)

Chronological plan. The Book of Joshua covers about twenty-seven years. Based on information about the age of Caleb (Deuteronomy 2:14; Joshua 14:7), the military campaigns against the Canaanites under Joshua's leadership lasted seven years. In that time span *Joshua took the entire land* (Joshua 11:23). Even after the end of those campaigns, however, there remained yet very much land to be possessed (Joshua 13:1). Joshua died at the age of 110 about 1380 BC (Joshua 24:29).

Biographical plan. Joshua is the main character in the book that bears his name. Like Moses, God prepared Joshua for eighty years before he became Israel's leader. His life began in Egypt as a slave. During the forty years in the wilderness Joshua was Moses' servant. It was during that period that he and eleven others were sent into Canaan as spies.

After Moses' death Joshua received his commission to lead Israel. This great man of God appears in three roles during the period of the Conquest. First, during Israel's campaigns against the Canaanites Joshua served as military superior — commander of the forces (chs. 1–12). Second, when the territory was being divided among the tribes, Joshua served as an advisor (chs. 13–22). Third, Joshua's last public appearance was in the role of a preacher exhorting his people to be faithful to the Lord (chs. 23–24). Joshua was in a position of leadership in Israel for about thirty years. Moses brought Israel out of bondage and gave them God's law. On the other hand, Joshua brought Israel into blessing and gave them God's land.

Others who play bit parts in the drama of the conquest are these:

❖ **Rahab,** a harlot in Jericho who cast her lot with the Israelites and found salvation (ch. 2).

❖ **Achan,** who stole some items from the spoils of Jericho and thereby caused Israel to experience a military setback (ch. 7).

❖ **Caleb**, who at age 87 was still looking for mountains to conquer (ch. 14).

❖ **Eleazar**, the high priest who assisted in the distribution of the land to the tribes (19:51).

❖ **Phinehas**, the priest who nearly started a civil war over what he perceived to be an infraction of God's law (ch. 22).

❖ **Adonizedek**, king of Jerusalem who organized the southern coalition to withstand Israel (ch. 10).

❖ **Jabin**, king of Hazor who organized a northern coalition to oppose Israel (ch. 11).

Geographically the activities in the Book of Joshua take place in four areas:

❖ Jordan River area (chs. 1–5)

❖ Southern Canaan (chs. 6–10)

❖ Northern Canaan (11:1–13:7)

❖ Greater Canaan (13:8–24:33): territory east and west of the Jordan.

Eternal Purpose

The purpose of the Book of Joshua is to show how God brought Israel into the Promised Land in fulfillment of his promise. The larger purpose of the book is to underscore the truth that *this is the victory that has overcome the world, even our faith* (1 John 5:4).

This book teaches the truth that victory and blessing come through obedience and trust in God. In this book God challenged Israel to attempt the impossible. He provided them with a faith-plan for accomplishing the mission. He blessed every effort that his people undertook in faith.

In some ways the Book of Joshua is the sequel to the five books of Moses. At the same time this book introduces a new section of the biblical library. The five books of Moses lead Israel *up to* Canaan; and Joshua complements these by leading Israel *into* Canaan. The next eleven books narrate Israel's history inside Canaan. Joshua introduces these books by describing the Israelite *settlement* in Canaan.

In the Book of Joshua God made good on a promise made to Abraham, Isaac, and Jacob. The patriarchs received the promise of abundant posterity and a fertile land. The fulfillment of the first promise is documented in the Book of Exodus; the Book of Joshua documents fulfillment of the second promise.

Anticipation

There is no personal messianic prophecy in the Book of Joshua; but there is a Christophany—a manifestation of Christ. He appeared to Joshua in the guise of the Captain of the Lord's host (Joshua 5:13-15; cf. Revelation 19:11-14). As such he gave to Joshua the battle plan for conquering Jericho (Joshua 6:2-5).

This book contains a major type (preview) of the kingdom of heaven. According to Hebrews 3-4, Canaan pictures the believer's present position and possession in Christ. Paul's letter to the Ephesians sets forth the parallels between ancient Canaan and the *heavenly realms* inherited by Christians. Canaan was the predestined inheritance of a chosen people (Genesis 13:14-15; Exodus 13:5). The "heavenlies" are the inheritance of Christians (Ephesians 1:18-22). There is, however, this difference. Canaan bestowed on the Israelites material blessings, while the "heavenlies" are equated with spiritual blessings.

Other parallels between physical Canaan and the "heavenlies" are these. First, Israel entered Canaan through a divinely appointed leader, Joshua (Joshua 1:6; 11:23; Deuteronomy 1:6). We enter the "heavenlies" through the work of Christ (Ephesians 1:18-22). There is, however, this contrast. The Old Testament Joshua carried a sword. The New Testament Joshua carried a cross.

Second, Canaan was a gift of God's grace received by Israel through obedient faith (Joshua 1:6-9). In this same manner New Testament believers inherit the "heavenlies" (Ephesians 2:5-8).

Third, possession of Canaan came as the result of a striking demonstration of divine power (Joshua 4:24; Deuteronomy 28:10). So also did possession of the "heavenlies" (Ephesians 1:19-23).

Fourth, Canaan was a scene of conflict (Joshua 10:1-4; Deuteronomy 7:1); so also are the "heavenlies" that we have inherited (Ephesians 6:12).

Keys

The key chapter in this book is Joshua 24. In the speech recorded in this chapter Joshua prepares the way for a critical transition in leadership.

Perhaps the key verse in the book is: *I will give you every place where you set your foot, as I promised Moses* (Joshua 1:3). This verse sets forth what the Book of Joshua is all about. Other passages nominated as key verses are these: 1:5-9; 23:3b-11; 24:14-15.

The key phrases in Joshua are: *the* LORD (222) and *king of* (71).

Key words in the book are *land* (87); *take/took* (57); *border* (56).

Special Features

Three points relating to the Book of Joshua are worth noting.

❖ The original name of the man Joshua was *Hoshea = salvation* (Numbers 13:8). Eventually the name was changed to *Yehoshua = Yahweh is salvation* (Numbers 13:16). He was also called *Yeshua*, a shortened form of *Yehoshua*. This is the equivalent of the Greek name *Iesous* (Jesus).

❖ Joshua, like Deuteronomy, records the death of its author.

❖ Just as recorded in Joshua 3, the waters of the Jordan backed up at Adam in 1927 for twenty-one hours. An earthquake caused one of the cliffs to tumble into the river.

HEAR

God speaks to us in the Book of Joshua. We must hear the message. You can sample the exciting material in this book by studying these outstanding chapters.

❖ Crossing the Jordan (Joshua 3)
❖ The walls came tumbling down (Joshua 6)
❖ A thief in the camp (Joshua 7)

Here are a few of the famous lines found in the Book of Joshua:

❖ *Be strong and courageous* (1:6, 7, 9, 18).
❖ *I will never leave you nor forsake you* (1:5; cf. Hebrews 13:5).
❖ *Choose for yourselves this day whom you will serve. . . . But as for me and my household, we will serve the* LORD (24:15).
❖ *I am still as strong today as the day Moses sent me out; I'm just as vigorous to go out to battle now as I was then* (14:11).
❖ *Now give me this hill country that the* LORD *promised me that day* (14:12).
❖ *The sun stopped in the middle of the sky and delayed going down about a full day* (10:13b).

7ᵗʰ Bible Book
Book of Judges
Israel's Dark Ages

The seventh book of the Bible is called *Judges* in both the Hebrew Bible and in the Greek and Latin Bibles. The biblical Judges were not black-robed judicial arbiters. They did not make laws or interpret laws. The biblical Judges were deliverers raised up by God to deal with Israel's oppressors.

This book contains twenty-one chapters, 618 verses, and 18,976 words.

There is a stark contrast between the Book of Joshua and the Book of Judges. The successes of Joshua have turned to failure. There are intermittent deliverances in this book; but the tone of Judges is predominately one of oppression and defeat. The former book rings with shouts of victory, freedom, and progress. Judges echoes with sobs of defeat, bondage, and decline. In Joshua Israel rejoices in possession of the land; in Judges Israel sighs under oppression in the land. The faithfulness of Israel in Joshua is offset by the faithlessness in the Book of Judges. In Joshua God's people were walking by faith; in Judges, they were living in the flesh.

Situation

The Book of Judges is written anonymously. Jewish tradition suggests that Samuel was the author. The facts support this tradition. Judges was composed after the death of Joshua (Judges 2:7) and after the days of the Judges (Judges 17:6; 18:1; 19:1; 21:25). The book was written before the seventh year of David (1002 BC), since the Jebusites still held Jerusalem (Judges 1:21; cf. 2 Samuel 5:6). Judges was written from a prophetic point of view (cf. Judges 3:7; 4:1).

Some think that Judges 18:30, which mentions the captivity of the land, rules out Samuel as author. The captivity of the land, however, could be the Philistine captivity, not the Assyrian captivity which occurred long after the time of Samuel. So the conclusion is that the Book of Judges was written about 1035 BC during the reign of Saul and just before the death of Samuel.

The background of Judges can be sketched in these brief sentences: The national campaign to conquer the land of Canaan lasted seven years. The individual tribes were required to eliminate the remaining pockets of Canaanite resistance. After the death of Joshua and the elders associated with him, the nation drifted into apostasy. With the invasion of Cushan-rishathaim, a king from Mesopotamia, the period of the Judges began.

Plan

Judges consists mainly of historical narrative. There is, however, one song (Judges 5) written by the prophetess Deborah. The book has been arranged in three main divisions that tell of Israel's decline, deliverances, and depravity.

❖ **Explanatory prologue** (1:1–3:6)

❖ **Sin/salvation cycles** (3:7–ch. 16)

❖ **Illustrative epilogue** (chs. 17–21)

The explanatory prologue describes Israel's sin (1:1–2:5) and consequent slavery (2:6–3:6). The heart of the book reports six oppressions of Israel and the rule of twelve Judges. A recurring pattern of rebellion, retribution, repentance, rescue, and rest is found in this section.

Clearly the focus of Judges is on the cycles. In the *rebellion* phase the Israelites turned to idolatry and abandoned God's law. The Lord sent against Israel *retribution* in the form of an enemy to oppress his people. In the *repentance* phase of each cycle Israel turned back to God, confessing its sin and begging for help. *Rescue* came in the person of a charismatic leader (a Judge) who defeated the oppressor. Deliverance was followed by a period of *rest* during which the Judge helped Israel remain faithful to the Lord. The tragedy is that in each repetition of this cycle the rebellion was more grievous and the oppression more severe.

The Book of Judges concludes with two stories that illustrate how deplorable conditions in Israel were after the death of Joshua. The first story tells how idolatry came to be practiced publicly in the land (chs. 17–18). The second story tells of an outrageous sexual atrocity and the bloody civil war that resulted from it (chs. 19–21).

The sin/salvation cycles in Judges have been carefully arranged in two triads. In each cycle there is at least one oppressor, one main Judge, and sometimes a lesser Judge or Judges about whom little is recorded. The pattern is set forth in the following chart.

First Triad of Cycles	Second Triad of Cycles
The Israelites did evil in the eyes of the LORD (3:7).	*The Israelites did evil in the eyes of the LORD* (6:1).
1. Cushan oppressed; Othniel delivered (3:7-11)	**4.** Midianites oppressed; Gideon, Tola, Jair delivered (6:1–10:5)
Again the Israelites did evil in the eyes of the LORD (3:12) **2.** Eglon oppressed; Ehud, Shamgar delivered (3:12-31)	*Again the Israelites did evil in the eyes of the LORD* (10:6) **5.** Ammonites & Philistines oppressed; Jephthah, Ibzan, Elon delivered (10:7–12:15)

Again the Israelites did evil in the eyes of the LORD (4:1) **3.** Jabin oppressed; Deborah delivered (4:1–5:31)	Again the Israelites did evil in the eyes of the LORD (13:1) **6.** Philistines oppressed; Samson resisted (13:1–16:31)

In the chart that follows the individual Judges are identified. Some pertinent information about the more important Judges is summarized.

Heroes of the Book of Judges			
Name	**Tribe**	**Identification**	**References**
1. Othniel	Judah	Caleb's nephew; old man	3:9-11
2. Ehud	Benjamin	Left-handed assassin	3:12-20
3. Shamgar	Foreigner ?	Used an ox goad	3:21
4. Deborah	Ephraim	Woman; judged Israel under a palm tree	4:4–5:31
5. Gideon	Manasseh	Defeated Midianites with 300 men	6:11–8:35
6. Tola	Issachar		10:1-2
7. Jair	Gilead	Thirty sons ruling thirty cities	10:3-5
8. Jephthah	Gilead	Made a rash vow	11:1–12:7
9. Ibzan	Judah	Thirty sons and thirty daughters	12:8-10
10. Elon	Zebulun		12:11-12
11. Abdon	Ephraim	Forty sons & thirty grandsons who rode on seventy donkeys.	12:13-15
12. Samson	Dan	Nazirite from birth	13:2–16:31

Eternal Purpose

The immediate purpose of Judges is to record the events of Israel's history from the death of Joshua to the founding of the monarchy. By so doing the author aimed to explain and defend the establishment of the monarchy. The deeper purpose of Judges is to teach the terrible consequences of disobedience and the wonderful potential of genuine repentance.

After following Israel to victorious heights in the Book of Joshua, we descend in the Book of Judges into a dark valley. Many tragic and sordid episodes are recorded in this book. The three centuries of the period of the Judges were Israel's dark ages. We cannot erase this tragic record of repeated failures. We can, however, learn from it. In no book of Scripture are the lessons more clearly set forth.

The key lesson in the book is that failure results from compromise. There are four examples of such compromise: 1) failure to drive all the Canaanites out of the land (ch. 1); 2) covenants or treaties with neighboring peoples (2:2); 3) intermarriage with unbelievers (3:6); and 4) idolatry (2:13; 3:6).

The Book of Judges underscores that no past experience of blessing removes the tendency to sin, or dispenses with the need of watchfulness against temptation. No position of honor or favor entitles one to sin with impunity. There is also, however, this lesson: for recovery from backsliding, however terrible, there is provision made in the mercy of God. Despite repeated failures, God remains willing to give his straying people new opportunities to "get it right."

A basic lesson in Judges can be discerned by placing two verses side by side:

Everyone did as he saw fit (17:6)   *Then the Israelites did evil in the eyes of the LORD* (2:11)

One can observe in Judges how God frequently uses what the world of that day counted as insignificant to accomplish his will. Othniel was an old man when he delivered Israel. Ehud was a left-handed man. (Lefties were viewed with suspicion in the ancient world). Cowardly Barak would only go into battle if Deborah were at his side. Gideon fought against tremendous odds with only three hundred men armed with lamps, jars, and trumpets. Shamgar's only weapon was an ox-goad. Judge Jephthah was an outcast and an outlaw. Samson defeated the Philistines with the jawbone of a donkey. It is clear that *God chose the foolish things of the world to shame the wise; God chose the weak things of the world to shame the strong* (1 Corinthians 1:27).

Anticipation

There is no direct predictive prophecy concerning the person and work of Messiah in the Book of Judges. One can, however, reflect on the deliverers in this book and see foregleams of the work of Christ. As Israel's Judges inflicted defeat on the enemies of God's people, so Christ struck a decisive blow against the forces of darkness when he died and rose from the dead. Israel's Judges brought interludes of rest to God's people; but Christ offers eternal rest to those who put their trust in him (Matthew 11:28). The deliverers in this book were flawed men; but Christ's deliverance is perfect because he is the sinless Savior.

Keys

The key chapter in the book is Judges 2. This chapter is a miniature of the entire book.

The key verse is this: *In those days Israel had no king; everyone did as he saw fit* (Judges 17:6).

The key phrase is *did evil in the eyes of the LORD* (7).

The key word in this book is *deliver* + cognates, which appears about forty-seven times.

Special Features

Here are some facts about the Judges that make this book stand out within the sacred collection.

❖ Not all of the Judges of Israel are mentioned in the Book of Judges. At least two — Eli and Samuel — are mentioned in 1 Samuel.

❖ Women are prominent in Judges. Their cunning and courage often exposed the men in their lives as weak, foolish, and cowardly. Deborah, the only female Judge, stands out. Other strong women in the book are Jael, Jephthah's daughter, Samson's mother and (on the evil side) Delilah.

HEAR

Our Lord speaks to us through the Book of Judges. We must hear him, but with a discerning ear. Here are some of the outstanding chapters in the book so you can sample what Judges has to say:

- ❖ Deborah's victory over Sisera (Judges 4)
- ❖ Gideon puts out the fleece (Judges 6)
- ❖ Gideon's victory with 300 men (Judges 7)
- ❖ Jephthah's thoughtless vow (Judges 11)
- ❖ Samson's marriage (Judges 14)

Here are a few of the famous lines in the Book of Judges:
- ❖ *I will place a wool fleece on the threshing floor* (6:37).
- ❖ *God has paid me back for what I did to them* (1:7b).
- ❖ *He [Samson] awoke from his sleep and thought, "I will go out as before and shake myself free." But he did not know that the LORD had left him* (16:20).

8ᵗʰ Bible Book
Book of Ruth
A Light of Faith in a Dark Age

The eighth book of the Bible is named after the most prominent person in the book. Ruth was a Gentile from the land of Moab who committed herself to the Lord. The book was probably written by Samuel. The genealogy at the end of Ruth *may* have been appended after the death of Samuel, during the reign of David.

The Book of Ruth contains four chapters, 85 verses, and 2,578 words.

Ruth is one of two biblical books to be named for a woman. The other such book is Esther. The two women stand in marked contrast. Ruth was a young Gentile woman who came to live among Hebrews and married a Hebrew farmer. Esther is a young Hebrew woman who lived among Gentiles and married a Gentile king. Both Ruth and Esther were great and good women. The Book of Ruth, however, is unique in this: it is the only instance in the Bible in which a whole book is devoted to a woman.

As a short story Ruth is a masterpiece. It is simple, natural, and complete. Ruth is a window to village life during the days of the Judges. After reading the stormy reports of bloodshed, crime, and rebellion in the previous book, this lovely story is like the calm that follows the storm. Simple piety pervades the story. There is a sense in this book of God's overruling providence. This is a story of love, devotion, and redemption displayed like a beautiful diamond against the black backdrop of the days of the Judges.

Situation

The opening verse of Ruth indicates that the setting for this book is the period of the Judges. Scholars generally believe that the events narrated in Ruth took place during the judgeship of Jair. While there is some dispute about the dates for this Judge, a recent study has placed him in the time frame 1109–1088 BC.

A famine in the region of Judah caused a family from Bethlehem to migrate to the land of Moab. While living there the father died, leaving his wife Naomi and two sons to fend for themselves without a breadwinner. The boys grew up and married two Moabite women. Then, however, the husbands also died. Naomi decided to return to Bethlehem where her husband had owned property. Ruth her widowed daughter-in-law insisted on going to Bethlehem with Naomi.

To support the two widows Ruth went out into the harvest fields with the poor to gather stalks that the harvesters left behind. The owner of the fields was a wealthy man named Boaz. This man was related to the husband of Naomi. The custom of the time was for a man to marry the widow of a close relative. When Boaz was confronted with this responsibility he made the legal arrangements and married Ruth.

Plan

Chronologically the Book of Ruth covers about twelve years. The book is organized into two major divisions. Chapters 1–2 relate how Ruth demonstrated her love for her mother-in-law Naomi. Chapters 3–4 relate how Ruth's love was rewarded.

Geographically the action in Ruth unfolds in four venues: Moab (ch. 1), Bethlehem's fields (ch. 2), a threshing floor (ch. 3), and a home in Bethlehem (ch. 4).

Eternal Purpose

The primary purpose of the Book of Ruth is to highlight an island of faith and integrity in a sea of corruption. Despite the prevailing apostasy of the nation some individuals were living godly lives. For example, the character, integrity, and piety of Boaz are outstanding. He demonstrated familiarity with the Mosaic Law. His personal walk with the Lord stands in marked contrast with the general ignorance, immorality, indifference, and idolatry of the times. The abiding lesson of this book is that God never leaves himself without a witness.

Ruth provides the vital link between the days of the Judges and the coming of David. The climax of the book is a genealogy that points forward to Bethlehem's baby. This genealogy is a striking way of bringing before us the continuity of God's purpose through the ages.

In a sense salvation is the theme of the Book of Ruth. Ruth's life was a series of reversals from hardship to blessing. Ruth was saved from poverty to wealth, widow to wife, childlessness to motherhood, foreigner to Israelite, and pagan to one who professed faith in the Lord.

Ruth's savior was Boaz, a "kinsman-redeemer." According to ancient custom, the closest relative of a widow could agree to redeem her from a life of poverty by marrying her, taking care of her, and giving her children to inherit the dead father's land. Boaz did not marry Naomi because she was too old to have children. He agreed, however, to marry Ruth and take care of both widows.

Anticipation

There is no prophecy directly predicting the coming of Messiah in Ruth. In the kinsman-redeemer Boaz, however, we have a picture of Christ. The similarities are these: First, like the *kinsman-redeemer* Christ is our blood relative. Second, like the kinsman-redeemer Christ had the wherewithal and willingness to purchase our forfeited inheritance.

Behind the story of Ruth is the genealogy of the Messiah. Ruth the Moabitess is seen no longer as the courageous stranger who came to Bethlehem. She is the woman whose great love for Naomi and devotion to Naomi's God put her into the direct line of the Messiah.

Keys

The key chapter in Ruth is chapter 4. In this chapter Boaz married Ruth. A child was born who became the ancestor of David, and ultimately of Christ.

The key verse is this: *Don't urge me to leave you or to turn back from you. Where you go I will go, and where you stay I will stay. Your people will be my people and your God my God* (1:16).

Special Features

These are some of the special features that make Ruth distinct in the sacred collection.

- ❖ Television personality Oprah Winfrey was named after Orpah, the daughter-in-law of Naomi who returned to Moab.

- ❖ Matthew says the "mother" of Boaz in the Book of Ruth was Rahab, the prostitute who helped the Israelite spies in Jericho. Matthew probably means that Rahab was an ancestress of David, and thus of Christ.

- ❖ Jews today read the Book of Ruth annually at the feast of Pentecost.

- ❖ Originally Ruth was a third appendix to the Book of Judges (following the two stories in Judges 17–21). Separation from the larger scroll made it easier to read these chapters at the feast of Pentecost. This separation took place sometime after the days of Josephus, the Jewish historian who wrote ca. AD 90.

- ❖ The Jews put the newly created book of Ruth in the third division of the Hebrew Bible among the so-called *Megilloth* (*Scrolls*). Each of these five small scrolls was read on a Jewish feast day. In the Greek Bible Ruth was returned to its original location following Judges.

- ❖ Ruth is one of four women who are mentioned in the ancestry of Christ. The other three — Tamar, Rahab, and

Bathsheba — have stained character. Scripture, however, has nothing negative to say regarding Ruth.

❖ Each chapter in this book contains a blessing pronounced by one person upon another. Believers have a right (and perhaps an obligation) to speak such blessings in God's name.

HEAR

God speaks in the Book of Ruth. We must hear his truth. It will take you about fifteen minutes to read this little book. Here are some of the outstanding verses you will find:

❖ *"The LORD bless him!" Naomi said to her daughter-in-law. "He has not stopped showing his kindness to the living and the dead" (2:20)*

❖ *And now, my daughter, don't be afraid. I will do for you all you ask. All my fellow townsmen know that you are a woman of noble character (3:11).*

❖ *Then Boaz announced to the elders and all the people, "Today you are witnesses that I have bought from Naomi all the property of Elimelech, Kilion and Mahlon. ¹⁰I have also acquired Ruth the Moabitess, Mahlon's widow, as my wife, in order to maintain the name of the dead with his property, so that his name will not disappear from among his family or from the town records. Today you are witnesses!" (4:9-10).*

❖ *So Boaz took Ruth, and she became his wife. Then he went to her, and the LORD enabled her to conceive, and she gave birth to a son (4:13).*

❖ *The women living there said, "Naomi has a son." And they named him Obed. He was the father of Jesse, the father of David (4:17).*

CHAPTER FIVE

FRAMEWORK BOOKS (2)
1 Samuel–2 Chronicles

Three double books report the history of Israel during the period of the Israelite monarchy. The history of the monarchy breaks down into four phases: the Single Kingdom, when all the tribes were united in the recognition of Saul, David, or Solomon; the Sister Kingdoms Period when the tribes were separated into two rival kingdoms, Israel in the north and Judah in the south; the Assyrian Period in which the surviving kingdom of Judah was under the thumb of the Assyrian Empire. The last eighteen years of the kingdom of Judah fall into the Babylonian Period when Nebuchadnezzar was ruler of the world. This history is outlined in the following chart.

Israel's Monarchy History			
Single Kingdom	Sister Kingdoms	Assyrian Period	Babylonian Period
1043 BC	931 BC	723 BC	605 BC
1 Sam 8–1 Kgs 11 1 Chr 10–2 Chr 9	1 Kgs 12–2 Kgs 17 2 Chr 10–28	2 Kgs 18–23 2 Chr 29–35	2 Kgs 24 2 Chr 36

9ᵗʰ & 10ᵗʰ Bible Books
Books of 1 & 2 Samuel
Birth & Expansion of the Kingdom

Originally the two books of Samuel were one book. For that reason we will treat them together in this survey. In the Hebrew Bible the books are named after one of the leading figures in the narrative. In the Greek Bible, however, the books were named *1 & 2 Kingdoms*. The Latin Bible referred to them as *1 & 2 Kings*. Some early English versions adopted this latter designation, at least as a subtitle for these books.

There may be a clue to the authorship of these anonymous books in 1 Chronicles 29:29. This verse reads: *As for the events of King David's reign, from beginning to end, they are written in the records of Samuel the seer, the records of Nathan the prophet and the records of Gad the seer.* Perhaps Samuel was the primary writer of 1 Samuel 1–16. The prophet Gad probably wrote 1 Samuel 17 through 2 Samuel 5:3 and the prophet Nathan 2 Samuel 5:4 through 1 Kings 3:28.

The book we call 1 Samuel contains thirty-one chapters, 810 verses and 25,061 words. The second Samuel book is a bit smaller: twenty-four chapters, 695 verses and 20,612 words.

Situation

The material that we now refer to as 1 & 2 Samuel was probably put together by Nathan just after the death of David in 971 BC.

Chronologically the early chapters of 1 Samuel overlap the judgeship of Samson in the Book of Judges (Judges 13–16). Samson was never able to inflict a decisive defeat on the Philistines for the two decades of his judgeship. Samuel was growing up at the Tabernacle in Shiloh during these years. When Samson died about 1049 BC the Philistine yoke had not yet been cast off.

A turning point came when the tribal elders requested that Samuel anoint a king for Israel. God always intended to give Israel a king. One of the blessings promised to Abraham and Jacob was that kings would come from their line (Genesis 17:6;

35:11). Moses gave laws anticipating kingship (Deuteronomy 17:14-20). Yet the request for a king was wrong for two reasons. First, Israel was "jumping the gun," failing to wait on the Lord to provide for them a king. Second, Israel insisted on having a king like all the nations.

Plan

The Samuel books contain mostly historical narrative. Also found in these books are prayers, songs (1 Samuel 2; 2 Samuel 22, 23), and lists (2 Samuel 21:15-22; 23:8-39).

The theme of 1 Samuel is *the birth of the kingdom*. The chapters of this book are organized into three major blocks:

❖ **Judgeship of Samuel** (chs. 1–7)

❖ **Kingship of Saul established** (chs. 8–15)

❖ **Kingship of David anticipated** (chs. 16–31)

The theme of 2 Samuel is *the expansion of the kingdom*. The pivotal chapter in this book is chapter 12, which relates David's terrible transgression with Bathsheba. The preceding chapters of this book relate David's *triumphs* (chs. 1–11), while the following chapters (chs. 13–24) report David's *troubles*.

Chronological plan. First Samuel covers about 108 years — from the birth of Samuel (ca. 1118 BC) to the death of Saul (ca. 1009 BC). Second Samuel focuses on the forty-year reign of David, first over Judah alone (chs. 1–4), then over all the tribes (chs. 5–24).

Geographical plan. The Samuel books focus primarily on the following venues: Shiloh (1 Samuel 1–7), Gibeah of Benjamin (1 Samuel 8–15), the wilderness of Judah (1 Samuel 16–31), Hebron (2 Samuel 1–4), and Jerusalem (2 Samuel 5–21).

Biographical plan. The Samuel books focus on four main characters: Eli, Samuel, Saul, and David. Their stories are interwoven.

Samuel was sent by God to deliver Israel when the nation's fortunes seemed almost hopeless. Spiritually and politically Israel was destitute at the end of Eli's judgeship. Samuel, the man of prayer (Jeremiah 15:1; Psalm 99:6), brought renewal, relief from oppression, and hope. Samuel was the last of the Judges (1 Samuel 7:6, 15-17) and the first of a new line of prophets (1 Samuel 3:20; Acts 3:26; 13:20).

Saul the son of Kish was anointed by Samuel as Israel's first king. He was a man with great potential for leadership. Saul proved himself, however, to be a man of folly (2 Samuel 26:21). His kingship was marked by blatant disobedience to God and insane jealousy of David.

David is said to be a man after God's own heart (1 Samuel 13:14). This does not mean that David was a perfect man. His life was stained by sin. Yet David always listened when God spoke. He is depicted as courageous in battle, devoted to God, and a charismatic leader of men. David was a man of decisive action, a poet, a generous foe, and a loyal friend.

There are three distinct phases of David's life: rise to power (1039-1009 BC) — thirty years, his rule over Judah (1009-1002 BC) — 7.5 years, and his rule over all Israel (1002-969 BC) — thirty-three years.

Eternal Purpose

The immediate purpose of the Samuel books is to relate the circumstances surrounding the founding of the monarchy in Israel and the expansion of the Israelite kingdom into a significant power. The ultimate purpose is to reveal the divine origin of the messianic house of David — the family through which the Messiah would come (2 Samuel 7:12f).

The purpose of a large chunk of the Samuel books is illuminated by a thirteenth-century Hittite document called *Apology of Hattusilus*. It is a defense of a new Hittite dynasty. This document suggests that it was customary for a new ruling family to defend its right to rule. The biblical author intends to defend the change of the ruling family from Saul the Benjamite to David the Judahite. He aims to establish the legitimacy of David and his line, and to defend their continuing right to the throne. As in the Hittite document the Samuel books present a detailed description of why the previous ruler (Saul) was disqualified. There is an emphasis in both reports on events leading up to the ruler taking the throne. Both reports affirm the piety of the new ruler. Both contain a summary of the new king's reign showing that God confirmed his choice by blessing the nation.

1 Samuel. The Samuel books are full of practical lessons for God's people. For example, 1 Samuel is a warning to leaders. Spiritual leaders must be "in tune" with God so that they can adequately discharge their responsibilities (3:1-10). Leaders are warned to act within the restrictions imposed upon them by the word of the Lord (13:1-10; 15:9-11). The measure of good leadership is demonstrated in one's ability to respond properly to trials (13:11-23; 15:9-31; 27:1-7; 30:1-20).

First Samuel also teaches a great deal about the place of prayer in the life of believers (1:10-28; 7:5-10; 8:5-6; 9:15; 12:19-23; 28:6).

The major divisions of 1 Samuel illustrate three great principles. The chapters dealing with Samuel the prophet underscore the truth that *God is spirit, and his worshipers must worship in spirit and in truth* (John 4:24). In the Saul chapters one sees illustrated the teaching that *whoever keeps the whole law and yet stumbles at just one point is guilty of breaking all of it* (James 2:10). The David chapters pound home the truth that *the plans of the* LORD *stand firm forever, the purposes of his heart through all generations* (Psalm 33:11).

2 Samuel. Without question the key theological thought in 2 Samuel is the promise of an everlasting dynasty for David (2 Samuel 7). On a more practical level, 2 Samuel emphasizes the believer's dependence on God (2:1; 5:3; 6:16, 21; 7:18; 8:6, 14; 12:16; 22:1). One can also glean from this book some notion of the awfulness of sin and the limits of forgiveness.

In 2 Samuel the biblical writer offers a very candid portrait of the strengths and weaknesses of David. God shows no respect of persons. The heroes of the Bible are not sanitized and whitewashed. The good, the bad, and the ugly episodes are there for all to examine.

Anticipation

The Samuel books contain three major announcements of the coming of Christ. The first is found in Hannah's song that celebrates the ultimate fairness of God. The song reaches a climax when Hannah speaks of worldwide judgment at which time *the LORD . . . will give strength to his king and exalt the horn of his anointed* (1 Samuel 2:10). The Hebrew term for *anointed* can be translated *Messiah*.

The second messianic prophecy comes from the lips of an anonymous prophet. He predicted the ultimate removal of the Aaronic priesthood and the rise of a faithful priest who will oversee a new priestly house (1 Samuel 2:35). The reference most likely is to Christ and the New Testament priesthood.

The third messianic announcement comes through Nathan the prophet. He assured David that God will give him an enduring dynasty. As long as there was a throne in Israel a descendant of David would sit on it. The throne and kingdom of David were to endure forever. The "foreverness" of this prediction points forward to that Son of David (Christ) who lives forever. He today sits upon the throne that David once occupied, namely, the throne of God (1 Chronicles 29:23).

Keys

The key chapters in the Samuel books are 1 Samuel 15 and 2 Samuel 7. The former chapter records the tragic disobedience of Saul and the announcement of the anointing of a king after God's own heart. The latter chapter narrates the everlasting covenant that God made with David concerning the throne.

The key verses in the books are these:

❖ *But the people refused to listen to Samuel. "No!" they said. "We want a king over us"* (1 Samuel 8:19).

❖ *Your [David's] house and your kingdom will endure forever before me; your throne will be established forever* (2 Samuel 7:16).

The key phrase in the Samuel books is *before the* LORD (29).
The key words are *king/kingdom* (339).

Special Features

Several interesting features distinguish the Samuel books from other biblical literature.

❖ Ichabod Crane, the vain and cowardly man who was terrorized by a headless horseman in *The Legend of Sleepy Hollow*, gets his name from a grandson of Eli.

❖ The two books of Samuel were originally one book. When the Old Testament was translated into Greek about 250 BC, the book was divided. Ancient Hebrew did not have vowel symbols; Greek requires vowels. The Greek translation practically doubled the size of the book, making it unwieldy on one scroll.

❖ William Faulkner's novel *Absalom, Absalom* [the story of a southern aristocrat who returned from the Civil War to find his son missing and his plantation ruined] was inspired by the tragic story of King David and his son.

❖ The first appearance of the word Messiah (*anointed one*) appears in 1 Samuel 2:10.

HEAR

God speaks in the Samuel books. We must hear. See if you can discern the voice of God speaking to your heart as you read this selection of chapters from these two books.

❖ Samuel and the Mizpah revival (1 Samuel 7)
❖ The people demand a king (1 Samuel 8)
❖ Saul's failure to obey God (1 Samuel 15)
❖ Samuel secretly anoints David (1 Samuel 16)
❖ David kills Goliath (1 Samuel 17)
❖ Saul and the witch of Endor (1 Samuel 28)
❖ David captures Jerusalem (2 Samuel 5)
❖ God's covenant promises to David (2 Samuel 7)
❖ David's sin with Bathsheba (2 Samuel 11–12)
❖ Absalom rebels against his father (2 Samuel 15–19)

Here are a few of the favorite lines in the Samuel books:

- ❖ *Long live the king* (1 Samuel 10:24).
- ❖ *To obey is better than sacrifice* (1 Samuel 15:22).
- ❖ *There is only a step between me and death* (1 Samuel 20:3).
- ❖ *I have acted like a fool* (1 Samuel 26:21).
- ❖ *I have sinned against the* LORD (2 Samuel 12:13). This was David's response to the prophet Nathan's accusation.
- ❖ *O my son Absalom! My son, my son Absalom! If only I had died instead of you – O Absalom, my son, my son!* (2 Samuel 18:33).

11ᵗʰ & 12ᵗʰ Bible Books
Books of 1 & 2 Kings
Glory & Decline of the Kingdom

The eleventh and twelfth books of the English Bible were considered one book in the Hebrew Bible. The book was named *Kings* after the first Hebrew word. When the book was translated into Greek it was divided into two books. These books were given the names *3 & 4 Kingdoms*, the previous two books being called *1 & 2 Kingdoms*. In the Latin Bible the books were called *3 & 4 Kings*.

Although 1 Kings has fewer chapters (22) it contains more verses (816) and words (24,524) than 2 Kings with twenty-five chapters, 719 verses, and 23,532 words.

Modern man finds it difficult to imagine what life under an Oriental monarchy was like. The monarchy period, however, is crucial in the unfolding story of redemption. For this reason the Book of Kings is pivotal in the library of sacred literature. Therefore, the culture gap must be bridged and the contents of this book mastered if one is going to show himself approved as a student of God's word. In these books we can trace the history of a nation from affluence and prestige to poverty and bondage.

Situation

Jewish tradition assigns the authorship of the books of Kings to the prophet Jeremiah. Believers are not obligated to defend Jewish tradition on such matters. Scholars, however, have noted much language affinity between the books of Jeremiah and Kings. No conclusive argument against Jeremiah's authorship has been raised.

The Kings material was penned shortly after the fall of Jerusalem in 586 BC. The last four verses are an appendix that had to be added at least twenty-five years later when former King Jehoiachin was released from captivity.

The background of the Kings material can be summarized like this: After ruling for some thirty-three years from his capital in Jerusalem, David became extremely ill. He apparently had made no public announcement about his successor, although in the palace it was generally known that Solomon was the king's choice. Adonijah, David's oldest surviving son, attempted to take advantage of his father's condition to steal the throne.

Plan

Kings consists mostly of narrative of different kinds—conversational narrative, reports, prophetic narrative, dream narrative, and historical exposition. The books contain a variety of speeches—political speeches, farewell speeches, messenger speeches, sermons, royal petitions, directional speeches, and prophetic oracles. One also finds in Kings prayers, poems, lists, chronological notices, obituaries, fables (2 Kings 14:9), building specifications, and letters.

Literary plan. The structure of the Books of Kings is indicated in the following chart:

1 Kings		2 Kings		
Focus on Solomonic Kingdom	Focus on Both Kingdoms	Focus on Northern Kingdom	Focus on Both Kingdoms	Focus on Southern Kingdom
1 King	7 Kings N 4 Kings S	3 Kings N	9 Kings N 7 Kings S	8 Kings S
1 Kgs 1–11	1 Kgs 12–22	2 Kgs 1–10	2 Kgs 11–17	2 Kgs 18–25
Strength	S t r u g g l e			Storm
Single Kingdom	**Sister Kingdoms**			**Surviving Kingdom**

Chronological plan. Solomon's reign lasted forty years. After his death, God's people divided into two kingdoms — Israel in the north, Judah in the south — for a period of about 210 years. During that time a total of nineteen kings ruled in the north while only eleven kings reigned in the south. After the destruction of the northern kingdom, Judah continued to survive for about 136 years. During this time eight descendants of David sat on the throne in Jerusalem.

Biographical plan. One king and two prophets are the superstars of the Kings material. The king is Solomon. The prophets are the E-team — Elijah and Elisha. In the northern kingdom there were two major kings — Jeroboam and Ahab (with his wife Jezebel). Five kings in the southern kingdom led national revivals. For that reason they are worthy of being named to the major players list: Asa, Jehoshaphat, Joash, Hezekiah, and Josiah.

Geographical plan. The action in Kings focuses on Palestine, much of the time divided between the two tiny sister kingdoms. Foreign nations that are mentioned prominently in these books are Egypt, Damascus (the Arameans), and the two Mesopotamian powers of Assyria and Babylon.

Eternal Purpose

The immediate purpose of the Kings books is to narrate the history of the Israelite kingdom from the death of David to the destruction of Jerusalem and the end of the monarchy. The deeper purpose of these books is to teach that obedience to the law of God brings prosperity while apostasy leads to judgment.

Divine government. The author of Kings never intended his work merely to be the cold recitation of facts. He intended rather to teach important theological and practical truths. This is history written, not from a civil, but from a religious point of view. Aided by the Holy Spirit, the author could see the hand of God at work in the period of the monarchy. It was spiritual rather than political lessons that he was trying to teach. For this reason he especially focuses his attention on the two crisis periods—the reigns of Ahab in the north and Hezekiah in the south.

Secondarily in Kings one can see in stark contrast failed government by man and the unfailing government by God. Theologically, Kings stresses that God rules history and orchestrates it for his own purposes. He uses various nations as his instruments of judgment for Israel's failure to keep the covenant with their God.

The writer of Kings gives considerable attention to the three great institutions that symbolize the presence of God among his people: the Temple, prophetism, and the Davidic dynasty.

Temple. The books of Kings underscore the supreme importance of God's plan for a central place of worship—the Temple. The writer regarded all worship outside Jerusalem as illegal. The Temple was not only a shrine, it was God's earthly palace.

Davidic promises. The promises to David are the red thread that runs through the history of the kings from Solomon to the exile. For the sake of David, God tolerated the reigns of some of David's wicked descendants. Despite human sin and failure God was faithful to the Davidic covenant (2 Samuel 7).

Prophetism. The role of prophets as God's ambassadors was crucial during the monarchy. Because of the presence of these prophets the disobedience of the people was inexcusable. God was justified in finally destroying Jerusalem and the Temple. Nearly a third of the material in Kings is devoted to a forty-year period covering the ministries of Elijah and Elisha. The E-team battled against the influence of Jezebel and the infiltration of the Baal cult.

Anticipation

There is no personal messianic prophecy in Kings. This book reminds us, however, that Jesus is the King of all kings. Solomon (in his royal role) and the Temple that he built have typological implications. We are invited to make a comparison between Jesus and Solomon when the Master said: *one greater than Solomon is here* (Matthew 12:42). Solomon's Temple was designed to set forth truths which are incorporated into the spiritual temple built by

Christ (1 Corinthians 3:16f; Ephesians 2:21; 1 Peter 2:5). The failures in the kingdoms of Israel and Judah created anticipation of a glorious kingdom ruled by an ideal king, even Jesus.

Keys

Chapter 12 is the key chapter in 1 Kings. It records how the glorious kingdom of Solomon split into two rival kingdoms (Israel and Judah).

Perhaps the key verses are these: *As for you, if you walk before me in integrity of heart and uprightness, as David your father did, and do all I command and observe my decrees and laws, ⁵I will establish your royal throne over Israel forever, as I promised David your father* (1 Kings 9:4-5). These words were spoken in a dream to Solomon after he had finished building God's Temple. The Lord renewed the promise of an eternal dynasty that he earlier had given to David (2 Samuel 7). The conditional element indicates that Solomon continued to enjoy divine favor only so long as he was faithful to the Lord.

The final chapter of 2 Kings is the key chapter in that book. It records the utter destruction of Jerusalem and the Temple in fulfillment of the threats of God's prophets over the centuries.

For 2 Kings perhaps the key verses are these: *So the LORD was very angry with Israel and removed them from his presence. Only the tribe of Judah was left, ¹⁹and even Judah did not keep the commands of the LORD their God. They followed the practices Israel had introduced* (2 Kings 17:18-19).

Several phrases appear repeatedly in the two books: *David his/my father* (21); *man of God* (55); *word of the LORD* (48); *are they not written* (41); and *in the sight of the LORD* (38).

As might be expected the key words in the books are *reign +* cognates (139), and *king/kings* (630).

Special Features

Here are a few of the unusual things pertaining to the books of Kings.

❖ Like the two Samuel books, the two Kings books were originally one book in the Hebrew Bible. The book was divided when it was translated into Greek about 250 BC.

❖ Nineteen consecutive evil kings ruled in Israel. Of the nineteen kings who ruled in the southern kingdom, five are said to have been good kings.

❖ Throughout its history (except for one brief usurpation by an evil woman) Judah was ruled by descendants of David. In the northern kingdom, however, the nineteen kings belonged to nine different dynasties or families.

❖ Comparing a ruthless and shameless woman to *Jezebel* is based on the biblical depiction of the wife of King Ahab.

❖ Legend says that the Queen of Sheba gave birth to a son by Solomon. This child supposedly became king of Ethiopia. The Falashas are a group of Ethiopian Jews who trace their roots to this king. The last of this line of kings was overthrown in 1974.

❖ The name of King Ahab's father, Omri, shows up in the ancient records of both the Moabites and the Assyrians. To the Assyrians Israel was known as *the land of Omri.*

❖ The only surviving image of a king mentioned in the Bible is that of King Jehu. He is depicted on a stone Assyrian monument bowing before his superior. Along with a list of the treasures that he gave to King Shalmaneser, Jehu's name appears on the monument.

❖ The Assyrian king Sennacherib has left for us his own account of his invasion of Judah in 701 BC. It augments the biblical account with many details left unrecorded in the Bible.

❖ To prepare for the invasion by the Assyrians, King Hezekiah ordered the construction of a water tunnel underneath the southeastern hill of Jerusalem (2 Kings 20:20). Water still flows there to this day. Jerusalem tourists are permitted to hike through this tunnel.

HEAR

You will be able to sample the material in the books of Kings by reading these outstanding chapters:

- ❖ Solomon's Temple dedication prayer (1 Kings 8)
- ❖ Israel rebels against Solomon's son (1 Kings 12)
- ❖ Elijah raises a widow's son (1 Kings 17)
- ❖ Confrontation on Mount Carmel (1 Kings 18)
- ❖ Elijah's departure in a chariot of fire (2 Kings 2)
- ❖ Cleansing of Naaman the leper (2 Kings 5)
- ❖ Hezekiah's faith crisis (2 Kings 18–19)

Here are some of the favorite lines found in the books of Kings:

- ❖ *He [Solomon] then gave an order: "Cut the living child in two and give half to one and half to the other."* (1 Kings 3:25).
- ❖ *How long will you waver [limp] between two opinions? If the* LORD *is God, follow him; but if Baal is God, follow him* (1 Kings 18:21).
- ❖ *Tell him: "One who puts on his armor should not boast like one who takes it off."* (1 Kings 20:11).
- ❖ *"Go on up, you baldhead!" they said. "Go on up, you bald-head!"* (2 Kings 2:23). Spoken to Elisha.
- ❖ *The driving is like that of Jehu . . . he drives like a madman* (2 Kings 9:20).

13ᵗʰ & 14ᵗʰ Bible Books
1 & 2 Chronicles
Focus on David and His Kingdom

The name *Chronicles* is derived from the first two Hebrew words of the book. Literally translated they mean *the affairs of the days*, i.e., *the events of the times*. In the Greek Bible these books were known as *1 & 2 Paraleipomenon*, which means *the things left out*. The Latin Bible adopted the Greek name for the books. Until recently Catholic Bibles followed the title from the Latin Bible. The more recent Catholic English translations, however, have adopted the title *Chronicles.*

Like the Samuel books and the Kings books the Chronicles books were originally one book in the Hebrew Bible. The Greek translators divided the book at the transition from the reign of David to that of his son Solomon.

The second book is considerably longer than the first. In 1 Chronicles there are twenty-nine chapters, 941 verses, and 20,369 words. In 2 Chronicles there are thirty-six chapters, 822 verses, and 26,074 words.

A casual glance at the Chronicles material indicates great similarity to the Samuel–Kings books. About one half of the material in Chronicles is repeated virtually verbatim from the earlier books. Many of the negative events of David's life (e.g., his adultery with Bathsheba) are not recounted. It was not the author's intention to whitewash David. Rather, he has drawn his material from a well-known painful history.

Chronicles offers a different perspective on Israel's history from that found in Samuel–Kings. The following chart indicates the difference in approach in these two bodies of material.

Perspectives on Israel's History	
Samuel–Kings	Chronicles
1. More Biographical	1. More Statistical
2. More Personal	2. More Official
3. Prophetic Standpoint	3. Priestly Standpoint
4. Focus on Two Kingdoms	4. Focus on Judah
5. Throne Emphasis	5. Temple Emphasis
6. Exposed Guilt	6. Encouraged Loyalty
7. Political History	7. Religious History

Situation

Ezra, the priest and scholar, generally is considered to be the author of Chronicles. The books are written from a priestly point of view. There is continuity in substance, viewpoint, and style with the Book of Ezra. In fact the opening verses of Ezra repeat the concluding words of 2 Chronicles.

Chronicles obviously was written in the postexilic era—during the days of Nehemiah, Malachi, and the Persian King Artaxerxes I. The last recorded event in the book is Cyrus's proclamation releasing the Jews from captivity in Babylon (539 BC). A list of high priests, however, indicates that the writer lived a bit later than 539 BC. Chronicles was probably completed between 450 and 425 BC.

After the captivity was over, the remnant in Judah needed to be reminded of such things as heritage, covenant, temple, the dangers of apostasy, and messianic hope in the Davidic line. These Jews needed every encouragement to rebuild their nation. Chronicles is a clear warning to the people never again to forsake the Temple and the worship of the Lord.

Plan

Chronicles can be described as historical narrative preceded by a lengthy (9 chs.) section of genealogies. To a lesser extent Chronicles also contains lists, songs, prayers, and speeches of various kinds.

First Chronicles contains two main divisions: genealogies (chs. 1–9) and David's reign (chs. 10–29). Second Chronicles also contains two main divisions: Solomon's reign (chs. 1–9) and the reigns of nineteen kings of Judah (chs. 10–36). The last nine verses of the book are in the nature of an epilogue.

Chronological plan. The genealogies section traces ancestry back to Adam at the beginning. The period of time covered in this expansive genealogy is impossible to compute. The David and Solomon sections each cover forty years. The section dealing with the kings of Judah following Solomon covers about 345 years. The epilogue refers to the edict of Cyrus that was issued about forty-eight years after removal of the last king of Judah.

Biographical plan. The narratives in Chronicles center around David, Solomon, and five subsequent kings: Asa, Jehoshaphat, Joash, Hezekiah, and Josiah. These five kings were the only kings of the southern kingdom that the writer evaluates as good.

The opening genealogies themselves are artfully constructed according to a pattern commonly used in ancient literature. The technical name for this pattern is *chiasmus*. The purpose of a chiastic structure is to highlight a particular narrative, or in this case, a genealogy. This is accomplished by balancing the material on either side of the center. Dorsey[2] has pointed out this chiastic arrangement in the Chronicles genealogies as follows:

a. Nontribal register of past ancestors (1:1-54).
  b. Royal tribe Judah; David's family (2:1–4:23).
    c. Peripheral tribes (4:24–5:26).
      d. **Center**: tribe of Levi (5:27–6:66).
      (center of center: priests (6:49-60)
    c'. Peripheral tribes (7:1-40).
  b'. Royal tribe Benjamin; Saul's family (8:1-40).
a'. Nontribal register of present returnees (9:1-34).
Addendum: genealogy of King Saul (9:35-44).
        (repeated from 8:29-38 as transition)

Geographical plan. The action in Chronicles takes place for the most part in Judah, and in Jerusalem in particular.

Eternal Purpose

Chronicles was written to preserve the record of priestly worship from Saul to Cyrus. We can see in these books a deeper purpose as well. Chronicles underscores the central role of worship in the life of God's people.

The Samuel–Kings books were written originally for Jews in exile. Chronicles served to explain to the exiles why they had been deported from their land. Considerable space is devoted to discussion of the sins of Israel (northern kingdom). Chronicles, however, was written for Jews who had returned from the exile. The returnees needed to be encouraged with the proof that their covenant with God was still in force. So Chronicles focuses on the godly heritage of Israel rather than on their sinful history. In so

---

[2] David Dorsey, *The Literary Structure of the Old Testament* (Grand Rapids: Baker, 1999) 146.

doing Chronicles furnishes a foundation upon which the remnant could rebuild their land and lives.

Chronicles almost totally ignores the northern kingdom except where the history of that kingdom intersects with the history of Judah. The writer seems to agree with Hosea that the northern tribes were no longer God's people. The few representatives of those tribes who did return home identified with the Judeans or Jews. Those citizens who were left behind when thousands were hauled off to distant Assyrian provinces became assimilated into foreign cultures when they intermarried with Assyrian pioneers.

The Jewish remnant faced hard times in Judea. They were sustained by God's solemn word that one day a great king from the line of David would rule again over God's people. The line of David had not been exterminated by the exile to Babylon. The Messiah was to come from this line. Under his reign the most glorious days of the house of David were still future. Furthermore, Chronicles implies that the Lord was still present with his people. The writer sees the rise of Cyrus, the fall of Babylon, and the Persian edict of liberation as the first steps toward the great future that the prophets had promised Israel.

In the world of the Chronicler the Temple was 1) the symbol of the unity of the nation, 2) the reminder of the nation's religious vocation, 3) the sign that the Lord was still with his chosen people, and 4) the focus of the true emphasis in the national life. The author of this book interpreted his nation's history in the light of that Temple. The presence of that holy house encouraged continued reconstruction. The Temple was a link to the past and a pledge of a glorious future.

Clearly Chronicles was intended to be a Temple history. The author carefully traces the history of that structure through its conception under David, its construction and consecration under Solomon, its corruption and cleansings under various kings of Judah, and its destruction by the Babylonians. He pays close attention to those kings who were Temple-oriented. He delights in exploring how each of these godly rulers responded to significant tests of faith.

Anticipation

There are no specific messianic prophecies in Chronicles. The promise made to David of an everlasting throne (1 Chronicles 17), however, finds ultimate fulfillment in David's descendant Jesus Christ. Emphasis on God's Temple points forward to the day when one who was greater than the Temple came to abide among us (Matthew 12:6).

Keys

The key chapter in 1 Chronicles is chapter 17. This chapter parallels 2 Samuel 7 in recording the covenant with David about the throne.

The key verse is this: *I will set him over my house and my kingdom forever; his throne will be established forever* (1 Chronicles 17:14).

In 2 Chronicles the key chapter is chapter 34. This chapter records the last and greatest of the five revivals of Judah, this one led by King Josiah.

The key verses in this book are these words spoken by King Jehoshaphat: *Have faith in the LORD your God and you will be upheld; have faith in his prophets and you will be successful* (2 Chronicles 20:20b).

Key phrases in the Chronicles books are these: *seek the LORD* (10); *house of the LORD* (90); *house of God* (34); *covenant of the LORD* (12); and *eyes of the LORD* (19).

The key words in the books are these: *David* (254), *Jerusalem* (145), *covenant* (30), and *temple* (13).

Special Features

Some of the unusual or outstanding features of the Chronicles books are these:

- ❖ Chronicles is the last book in the Hebrew Bible.
- ❖ In the Greek Old Testament Chronicles was divided into two books, and placed after the two books of Kings.
- ❖ The one recorded time in the Bible when a person is reported to pray to God while seated is found in 1 Chronicles 17:16-27.

❖ The Book of Psalms contains the poems of Asaph. Chronicles identifies this Asaph as the man David appointed to play music and sing praises to the Lord in the Temple (1 Chronicles 16:4).

❖ The genealogies in 1 Chronicles 1–9 cover the time from Adam to David. Since the books of Chronicles are the last books of the Hebrew Bible, the genealogies in chs. 1–9 are a preamble to the genealogy of Christ in the Gospel of Matthew.

❖ If one includes the genealogies that extend back to Adam, Chronicles touches upon more history than any other Old Testament book.

HEAR

In the books of Chronicles God speaks. We must hear. Here are some of the outstanding chapters of these books for you to sample.

❖ David becomes king (1 Chronicles 11)
❖ The ark moved to Jerusalem (1 Chronicles 13–15)
❖ Solomon dedicates the Temple (2 Chronicles 6–7)
❖ Revolt against Solomon's son (2 Chronicles 10–11)
❖ Hezekiah faces the Assyrians (2 Chronicles 32)
❖ Discovery of a lost book of law (2 Chronicles 34)

Some of the significant sentences in the books of Chronicles are these:

❖ *Give thanks to the* Lord, *for he is good; his love endures forever* (1 Chronicles 16:34).

❖ *If my people, who are called by my name, will humble themselves and pray and seek my face and turn from their wicked ways, then will I hear from heaven and will forgive their sin and will heal their land* (2 Chronicles 7:14).

❖ *For the eyes of the* Lord *range throughout the earth to strengthen those whose hearts are fully committed to him* (2 Chronicles 16:9).

CHAPTER SIX

FRAMEWORK BOOKS (3)

Ezra–Esther

The history of Israel prior to the monarchy is narrated in three books (Joshua, Judges, Ruth). The monarchy history is related in the three double books of Samuel, Kings, Chronicles. So also the history of God's people after the monarchy disappeared is reported in a trio of books: Ezra, Nehemiah, and Esther. The third book in the trio is not in chronological order. It is a focus or sidestep book. Chronologically the events in the Book of Esther took place in the historical gap between chapters 6 and 7 of Ezra.

15ᵗʰ Bible Book
Book of Ezra
Restoration of the Nation

In the Hebrew Bible the fifteenth book of the Old Testament is named after the leading figure in the last four chapters of the book. The name Ezra means *help*. The Greek and Latin versions adopted the same name.

The book contains ten chapters, 280 verses, and 7,441 words.

The author of this book is Ezra. The text describes him as a priest and a scribe or scholar. He was commissioned by the Persian King Artaxerxes to teach and enforce God's law in the

Persian provinces beyond the Euphrates River. Much of the book is in the first person (7:28–9:15). Furthermore, Ezra 1:1 connects the Book of Ezra with 2 Chronicles. Jewish tradition is consistent in assigning this material to Ezra.

Situation

The background for the Book of Ezra is set forth in the first sentence of the book. The Hebrews had been in exile for *seventy years*. Now they were about to be released. God had raised up a new king, Cyrus king of Persia, *in order to fulfill the word of the* LORD *spoken by Jeremiah*. Cyrus conquered Babylon in 539 BC. The Lord moved the heart of Cyrus to issue a proclamation that allowed Israelite captives to return home.

Between chapters 6 and 7 of Ezra there is a historical gap of about fifty-eight years. Ezra himself arrived in Jerusalem in the fifth month of the Persian King Artaxerxes' seventh year or 457 BC (Ezra 7:8). The last recorded event in Ezra is the implementation of the findings of a divorce court in the tenth month, presumably of the seventh year of Artaxerxes (Ezra 10:16).

Plan

Ezra consists of narrative with lists, prayers, and royal decrees inserted. The material is arranged in two major divisions: *reconstruction* of the Temple (chs. 1–6) and *restoration* of the law (chs. 7–10). These two divisions of the book focus on the first two major returns of the Jews from Babylon. In the first division the prophets Haggai and Zechariah were the encouragers; in the second division the encourager is the scribe Ezra.

Chronological plan. The Book of Ezra covers about eighty years of the history of the Jews following the Babylonian exile. It describes the history of God's people from their first return from Babylon under King Cyrus (538 BC) to their second return under King Artaxerxes (457 BC). Ezra's history begins with a restoration decree of the king and concludes with a separation decree of a divorce court. In terms of Persian kings the material breaks down like this:

Cyrus (539–529 BC)	Ezra 1–3
Cambyses (529–522 BC)	Silence
Darius (521–486 BC)	Ezra 4–6
Xerxes (486–465 BC)	Ezra 4:6-7
Artaxerxes (464–424 BC)	Ezra 7–10

Three of these Persian kings were particularly instrumental in bringing about the restoration of the people of God. King Cyrus issued a formal decree inviting the Jews to return to Jerusalem and to rebuild the Temple. Decades later, Darius brushed aside non-Jewish opposition to the rebuilding program. He confirmed the earlier edict of Cyrus encouraging the Jews to rebuild their Temple. Finally, Artaxerxes encouraged Jews who still remained in Babylon to return home. He gave money and supplies to any who wished to go back to Canaan.

Biographical plan. Ezra stresses the roles of five great leaders: Zerubbabel, the first governor. He led in the effort to rebuild God's Temple; Joshua, the high priest who oversaw the Temple reconstruction project; Haggai and Zechariah, two prophets who encouraged the Temple work; and Ezra, who taught the returnees God's law.

Geographical plan. The focus of Ezra is on events in the Persian province of Judea.

Eternal Purpose

The immediate purpose of Ezra is to record the early history of the postexilic community. The deeper purpose is to record the fulfillment of God's promise to restore his people to the land of Canaan.

The Book of Ezra stresses one essential truth: God's Temple and God's word are essential to God's program in this world. Even before Nehemiah came to rebuild the city of Jerusalem, Zerubbabel rebuilt the Temple and Ezra restored the law. National reconstruction must begin with God.

The history of the nation Israel began with the account of how the Israelites came out of exile in Egypt. The Book of Ezra reports how the descendants of those Israelites returned from exile in Babylon. Nearly a thousand years separate these two exiles and exodus movements. Both events were predicted long before they occurred (Genesis 15:13-14; Jeremiah 25:11-12; 29:10-11). The first and famous exodus involved multiple times the number of people that participated in the exodus from Babylon. Yet, Scripture regards the second exodus to be of greater significance (Jeremiah 16:14f.). The reason is that the return from Babylon was the first step in the gathering of God's people that culminated in the work of Christ.

In the opening six chapters of Ezra one can trace several steps in the restoration of Israel that illustrate the process by which sinners can be reconciled with God. First, the sinners came back to the Lord (chs. 1-2). Second, rebuilding the altar (3:1-6) points to a restoration of fellowship with God. Third, the work of rebuilding the Temple (3:8-13) recognizes the importance of regular worship. Fourth, the obstacles encountered by the returnees (ch. 4) illustrate how the faith of believers is constantly tested. Fifth, God raised up prophets for his people (5:1-6:14), pointing to the need for faithful preaching in the lives of believers. Finally, the work of Temple reconstruction was completed (6:15-22). Faith ultimately wins the victory!

Anticipation

There is no explicit messianic prediction in the Book of Ezra. This book reveals, however, that God continued to fulfill his promises by preserving the royal line of David. The reconstruction of the Temple and reinstitution of the priestly rituals helped to keep before the people the basic principles that undergird the Christian system. Every sacrifice offered on the restored altar pointed forward to the final and perfect sacrifice of Christ on the cross.

Keys

The key chapter in the Book of Ezra is chapter 6. This chapter records the completion and dedication of the second Temple.

The key verse in the book is this: *For Ezra had devoted himself to the study and observance of the Law of the* LORD, *and to teaching its decrees and laws in Israel* (Ezra 7:10).

The key phrase is *house of the* LORD (9).

Among the key words are *Jerusalem* (44), *work* (10), and *build* (7).

Special Features

Some oddities, peculiarities, and features of the Book of Ezra that set this book apart from the others in the sacred collection are the following:

- ❖ The first two verses of Ezra repeat the last two verses of 2 Chronicles.
- ❖ Ezra includes some official Persian messages written in the Aramaic language, the official language of the Persian Empire.
- ❖ In the Hebrew Bible Ezra and Nehemiah were considered one book. The first known writer to speak of them as separate was the Christian scholar Origen in the third Christian century.

HEAR

Some of the outstanding chapters in the Book of Ezra are these:

- ❖ Temple foundations are laid (Ezra 3)
- ❖ Returnees encounter opposition (Ezra 4)
- ❖ Ezra confronts a marriage problem (Ezra 10)

Two of the favorite lines found in the Book of Ezra are these:

- ❖ *Let the temple be rebuilt* (Ezra 6:3).
- ❖ *According to their ability they gave to the treasury for this work* (Ezra 2:69).

16th Bible Book

Book of Nehemiah

Reconstruction of the Nation

The sixteenth book of the Bible is named after its chief character and author *Nehemiah*. The name means *the LORD has comforted*.

The Book of Ezra deals primarily with the religious restoration of Judah. Nehemiah is concerned with Judah's physical, political and geographical restoration. The book shows the presence of God with his people as they return to their homeland.

The Book of Nehemiah contains thirteen chapters, 406 verses, and 10,483 words.

Situation

Nehemiah wrote his memoirs early in his second term as governor of the Persian province of Judea. This second term of office began in (or slightly after) 432 BC, the thirty-second year of the Persian king Artaxerxes (Nehemiah 13:6).

Nehemiah began his career as a cupbearer to the Persian King Artaxerxes in Susa (in modern Iran). News came from Judea that the walls of the city of Jerusalem had been broken down. It seems that Ezra had exceeded his authority by attempting to rebuild those walls. The king ordered the regional enemies of the Jews to tear down the walls (Ezra 4:11-23). About twelve years later news reached Nehemiah in Persia about these developments. Because of his personal relationship with the king, in 445 BC Nehemiah secured permission to return to Jerusalem to rebuild the walls. He was also given a twelve-year appointment as Judean governor.

Nehemiah proved to be a dynamic leader. He demonstrated courage, compassion for the oppressed, integrity, godliness, and selflessness. Nehemiah refused to exercise his right to tax the people for the support of his administration. He even fed some indigent Jews at his own expense. Nehemiah was a dedicated layman whose obsession was the security of God's people. He was stalwart in resisting opposition and timely in encouragement. He was strong in prayer. Nehemiah never failed to give all the glory and credit to God.

Plan

From the literary standpoint Nehemiah has two divisions: *restoration* of Jerusalem (chs. 1–7); and *reforms* among God's people (chs. 8–13). The first division focuses on security, the second on separation or holiness. In the first seven chapters Nehemiah alone is the encourager, in the second he is joined by Ezra.

Chronologically the Book of Nehemiah covers about thirteen years, 445–432 BC. The first twelve chapters, however, focus on less than a year. The last chapter of the book describes events that happened over a few months after Nehemiah returned from Babylon with an appointment to a second term as governor. So chronologically the Book of Nehemiah has two divisions: Nehemiah's first governorship (chs. 1–12) and his second governorship (ch. 13).

In terms of practical values the book breaks down into three divisions: leadership principles (chs. 1–7), spiritual principles (chs. 8–10), and moral/social principles (chs. 11–13).

Eternal Purpose

The immediate purpose of Nehemiah is to continue the history of those who returned from Babylon. In the previous book the focus was on the rebuilding of the Temple; here the focus is on Jerusalem. The deeper purpose of Nehemiah is to demonstrate how leaders can accomplish great things for God in spite of determined opposition.

No portion of the Old Testament provides Christians with greater incentive to zeal for God's work and passion for God's word than the Book of Nehemiah. The book stresses that believers must *battle* as well as *build*. Opportunities for kingdom advancement always engender opposition. Open doors are always obstructed by adversaries (1 Corinthians 16:9). When Christians rise up to build, the enemy will rise up to tear down. In spiritual work there can be no triumph without trouble, no crown without a cross.

The perceptive reader does not see in Nehemiah merely a rebuilding of walls and gates. The truths of the book can apply to the building up of the walls of the city of God within every human heart and every nation of mankind. The book is full of many gems of teaching that encourage and instruct those who labor today to build up the walls of spiritual Zion, the kingdom of God.

Another emphasis of the book is often overlooked. Nehemiah was a man of prayer. This man demonstrated a balance of dependence and discipline, prayer and planning. His prayers were generally short but fervent.

Anticipation

There is no personal, direct messianic prophecy in the Book of Nehemiah. One is reminded by the building efforts of Nehemiah, however, that Christ came to build the heavenly Jerusalem (Galatians 4:25f).

Keys

The key chapter in Nehemiah is chapter 9. In this chapter the Jews reaffirmed their commitment to their covenant with God after they had built the walls of Jerusalem.

Perhaps the key verse is this: *I [Nehemiah] also told them about the gracious hand of my God upon me and what the king had said to me. They replied, "Let us start rebuilding." So they began this good work* (2:18).

Key words include *Jerusalem* (38), *wall* (32), and *work* (20).

Special Features

Some of the special features of the Book of Nehemiah are these:

- ❖ In the Hebrew Bible Ezra–Nehemiah was regarded as one book. The separation occurred in the Latin Vulgate in the fourth Christian century. Not until 1448 was the division into two books reflected in the Hebrew Bible.
- ❖ Women joined men in helping to rebuild Jerusalem's walls (Nehemiah 3:12).
- ❖ Nehemiah had to "draft" volunteers to occupy Jerusalem once the walls were rebuilt. This was done by casting lots.
- ❖ Several of the characters in Nehemiah are mentioned in documents outside the Bible. These include Sanballat, Tobiah, and Nehemiah's brother Hanani.

❖ The Persian city of Susa, where Nehemiah served as cupbearer, is the same setting for the story of Esther, the next book of the Bible.

❖ Queen Esther was King Artaxerxes' stepmother. It is possible that she was instrumental in the appointments of Ezra and Nehemiah to their respective positions in the Persian government.

❖ Under the leadership of Nehemiah, the Jews accomplished in fifty-two days what had not been done in the ninety-four years since the first return under Zerubbabel, that is, rebuild Jerusalem's walls.

❖ Jews brave enough to return to the homeland are doubly honored by being listed in Nehemiah 7 as well as Ezra 2.

HEAR

You can sample the contents of the Book of Nehemiah by reading the following chapters:

❖ Nehemiah returns to Jerusalem (Nehemiah 1–2)
❖ Jerusalem's walls rebuilt (Nehemiah 3–6)
❖ Nehemiah deals with abuses (Nehemiah 13)

Here are three outstanding verses in the Book of Nehemiah:

❖ *The people worked with all their heart* (Nehemiah 4:6).
❖ *They read from the Book of the Law of God, making it clear and giving the meaning so that the people could understand what was being read* (Nehemiah 8:8).
❖ *The joy of the* LORD *is your strength* (Nehemiah 8:10).

17ᵗʰ Bible Book
Book of Esther
Preservation of the Nation

The seventeenth book of the Bible has the Persian name of the heroine: *Esther* = *star*. The maiden's Hebrew name was *Hadassah* =

myrtle (2:7). The Greek and Latin Bibles use the Persian name as the title for the book, except that in Latin the queen's name is spelled *Hester*. One could argue that the book has been misnamed. Actually this book speaks of Mordecai (*Mawr'-dih-ki*) more often than it speaks of Esther.

Esther is the second of two biblical books to be named after a woman. The first was Ruth. The two women are very different. Ruth was a Gentile woman who married a Jew. Esther was a Jewish woman who married a Gentile. The two books named for women do have the same function in the sacred collection. This book, like the book of Ruth, is a focus or sidestep book. It does not advance the history beyond the closing event of Nehemiah. The book relates incidents that transpired before the history of Nehemiah and even before the last four chapters of Ezra.

Esther is a small book. It has but ten chapters, 167 verses, and 5,637 words.

Situation

The author of the Book of Esther is not known. On the basis of similarity of writing style, some have suggested that Ezra or Nehemiah wrote it. Others have proposed Mordecai or even Esther herself. The book was written during or shortly after the reign of the Persian King Xerxes (485–465 BC).

Chronologically the events in Esther fit between chapters 6 and 7 of Ezra. Several thousand Jews had returned to the homeland under the leadership of Zerubbabel about 538 BC. After the completion of the Temple in 516 BC no more is recorded about the activities of the remnant in Judea until 457 BC when Ezra returned to Jerusalem. The Book of Esther records one important episode in the life of the Jewish community that remained behind in the lands of the exile.

The ten chapters of Esther cover ten years. The opening banquet scene transpired in the third year of King Xerxes, 483 BC. The closing scene — the institution of the Feast of Purim — occurred in 473 BC. The following chart displays the chronological placement of the book within the biblical history of the period. The dark gray areas indicate years that are a blank in the biblical record.

Temple Finished	Darius	REIGN OF KING XERXES 485–465				Ezra's Return
Ezra 6:15	33 Years	Vashti Deposed 483	Esther Crowned 478	Purim Feast 473	15 Yrs	Ezra 7:9
516 BC		10 Years ←——————→ BOOK OF ESTHER				457 BC

Plan

The Book of Esther consists primarily of historical narrative, interspersed with royal decrees. The storyline centers on a crisis in which the Jewish people throughout the Persian Empire faced extermination. A twofold division of the material is most appealing: crisis anticipated (chs. 1–5); and crisis alleviated (chs. 6–10). In the former section the Jews are threatened; in the latter they are spared because of the brave intervention of Esther. A threefold breakdown of the material is also appealing: plot formed (chs. 1–3), plot fought (chs. 4–5), and plot foiled (chs. 6–10).

Those who are gastronomically oriented may notice that the Book of Esther focuses on banquets. Four are mentioned in the ten chapters: the king's feast (chs. 1–3), Esther's two feasts (chs. 4–7), and the Jews' feast (chs. 8–10).

Biographical plan. The Book of Esther focuses on three main characters. *Mordecai* was a crusty old Jew who had secured for himself the trusted position as one of King Xerxes' gatekeepers. Because of his loyalty to the crown he was promoted to prime minister.

Esther was Mordecai's cousin. She competes in a royal selection process and thereby becomes a favored wife of King Xerxes. Esther used her influence to expose a plot to exterminate the Jews.

Haman, the Persian Hitler, is the villain of the book. When he was elevated to prime minister he could not stand the fact that Mordecai refused to bow to him. Because of his personal hatred of one Jew, Haman purchased royal permission to exterminate all Jews in the Persian provinces on a set date. In the end his true motives were exposed. Haman was hung from the gallows he had intended for Mordecai. At that point the Jew Mordecai replaced Haman as prime minister.

Esther with its unexpected and ironic plot twists is one of the best-written short stories in all of ancient literature. In fact, it's so well written that some people think it is fiction—just too good to be true. Yet increasing evidence has come to light that the characters of this book were historical persons. The depiction of life in the Persian Empire fits what is known about the times of King Xerxes.

Geographical plan. The story of Esther is set in Susa, one of the capitals of the Persian Empire early in the reign of King Xerxes. The ruins of Susa are found in the modern country of Iran. The Persian palace of Susa, where Esther lived, has been unearthed by archaeologists. It covered more than twelve acres—nearly as big as Jerusalem was in David's day, and about half as big as the inside of a large shopping mall today.

Eternal Purpose

The immediate purpose of the Book of Esther is to show how a host of Jews living in exile were saved from being exterminated by the hand of a Gentile enemy. The deeper purpose of the book is to demonstrate the overriding providence of God in the affairs of men.

The most distinguishing feature of the Book of Esther is the absence of the name of God. In fact, there is no reference to any overt religious act in the book, unless one counts fasting as such. This nonmention of God in the story has been a problem in Jewish circles. Some ancient rabbis argued that this book should not be included in the sacred collection because of this omission. Martin Luther went so far as to say that he wished the book did not exist! Yet surely to find a problem in this nonmention of God is to miss what above all else the book intends for us to see.

How can a book that does not even mention God's name contribute to our understanding of the Lord? In this regard the old English pastor/scholar Matthew Henry made a cogent observation: "If the name of God is not here, his finger is." In this book believers learn that God is present even where his name is not heard. Another possibility is that God did not permit his name to be associated with Jews that did not have the courage and/or faith to migrate back to the Promised Land with their brethren.

The Book of Esther is the Scripture's clearest example of the doctrine of providence. God, although hidden from our view, works through circumstances and human choices to fulfill his purposes. Esther teaches us that the invisible God reveals himself in everyday life as well as in world events. This book implies that its readers should praise the Lord for his unfailing watch care.

Another purpose of the Book of Esther is to set forth one of the ugliest facts of human history—anti-Semitism. No century has been free of it. Through the ages Jews have been hated, persecuted, driven over the face of the earth, exiled, and killed. Like a smoldering fire, the flame of anti-Jewish bigotry bursts forth anew in the most unexpected places. Even enlightened Europe had its Buchenwald and Dachau where Jews by the millions were exterminated. The Jewish state of Israel even to this day is surrounded by terrorist states determined to drive the Jews into the sea. Yet the Book of Esther teaches us to celebrate, not only the marvelous preservation of the physical descendants of Abraham, but the survival of his spiritual descendants—Christians—as well.

Anticipation

There are no specific predictions or typology in the Book of Esther. Yet preparation for the coming of the Messiah continued by way of the preservation of the messianic people.

Keys

The key chapter in Esther is chapter 8. This chapter recounts how the Jews were saved from annihilation by the revised decree of King Xerxes.

The key verse in the book is this: *For if you remain silent at this time, relief and deliverance for the Jews will arise from another place, but you and your father's family will perish. And who knows but that you have come to royal position for such a time as this?* (Esther 4:14). These words were spoken to a reluctant Esther by her cousin and mentor Mordecai.

The key phrase in the book is *gave a banquet* (8 times with variation).

The key words are *Jew/Jews* (55 out of 76 times in the entire Old Testament).

Special Features

Here are some stand-out features of the Book of Esther:

- ❖ In the Hebrew Bible Esther is included as one of the five scrolls of the *Megilloth*. It is read at the winter Feast of Purim which celebrates the events recorded in this book.
- ❖ In the Greek Old Testament Esther was placed last among the historical books where it appears in the English Bible today.
- ❖ As noted above, the Book of Esther does not mention the name of God. Nor is there mention of prayer, sacrifice or any other worship practices.
- ❖ When the Jews read aloud the story of Esther during the feast of Purim, they boo, hiss, stomp their feet and jeer whenever Haman's name is read (some fifty times in the book).
- ❖ Because of the secular nature of this book, some rabbis raised questions about whether it should remain in the sacred collection. The greatest rabbis, however, supported the canonicity of the book.
- ❖ Esther is the only book in the Bible named after a *Jewish* woman.
- ❖ To overcome embarrassment that God is not mentioned in the book, Jews in the intertestamental period wrote certain additions to the Book of Esther that mention God frequently. These are part of the Catholic Book of Esther.

❖ Among the famous Dead Sea Scrolls, fragments of every Old Testament book were found except Esther.

HEAR

Some of the outstanding chapters in Esther are these:
  ❖ A queen who loved honor (Esther 1).
  ❖ A prime minister's pride humbled (Esther 6).
  ❖ Hanged on his own gallows (Esther 7).

Some famous lines in the book are these:
  ❖ *For the queen's conduct will become known to all the women, and so they will despise their husbands* (1:17).
  ❖ *Haman looked for a way to destroy all Mordecai's people, the Jews, throughout the whole kingdom of Xerxes* (3:6).
  ❖ *When he [Xerxes] saw Queen Esther standing in the court, he was pleased with her and held out to her the gold scepter that was in his hand* (5:2).
  ❖ *"A gallows seventy-five feet high stands by Haman's house. He had it made for Mordecai, who spoke up to help the king." The king said, "Hang him on it!"* (7:9).

CHAPTER SEVEN

FAITH BOOKS (1)

Job–Psalms

We have previously surveyed the five Old Testament Foundational Books and the twelve Framework or Historical Books. With this chapter we begin to explore a new shelf in the biblical library — the Faith Books. The five books on this shelf aim to help believers develop a stronger faith. Some refer to these books as devotional literature. Others prefer the terminology experiential literature, because these five books focus on the human experience.

At least nine individuals are named as contributing material to the shelf of Faith Books. Three of the contributors are well known: Moses, David, and Solomon. The remaining six contributors are Asaph, sons of Korah, Heman, Ethan, Agur, and King Lemuel.

Aspiration for Christ		
Book	Theme	Lesson
Job	Faith under Trial	Faith clings to God regardless of circumstances
Psalms	Faith in Various Circumstances	God is praiseworthy in all situations
Proverbs	Faith the Foundation of Wisdom	God is practical
Ecclesiastes	Faith the Key to Meaning	God gives meaning to life
Song of Solomon	Faith Expressed in Love	God smiles on steadfast love

Most of the Faith Books were composed during the Single Kingdom Period of Old Testament history, about one thousand years before Christ. An overview of the faith shelf with the themes and lessons for each book is displayed in the chart on the preceding page.

Since the books on the Faith shelf are essentially poetic books, a brief word about the basic types of Hebrew poetry is in order. The key to Hebrew poetry is neither rhyme nor rhythm; it is *parallelism* of thought. There are three major types of Hebrew poetry: In *synonymous* parallelism the second line repeats the thought of the first in slightly different words. For example:

> *The earth is the LORD's, and everything in it,*
> *the world, and all who live in it.* (Psalm 24:1)

In *antithetic* parallelism the second line offers a contrast to what is said in the first line. For example:

> *For the LORD watches over the way of the righteous,*
> *but the way of the wicked will perish.* (Psalm 1:6)

Synthetic or *constructive* parallelism designates a wide range of poetic verses in which the second line builds on the thought of the first line. The second line may complete the thought of the first line. For example:

> *I have installed my King*
> *on Zion, my holy hill.* (Psalm 2:6)

In synthetic parallelism the second line of a verse may state a comparison or express a value judgment. For example:

> *Better a meal of vegetables where there is love*
> *than a fattened calf with hatred.* (Proverbs 15:17)

The second line in synthetic parallelism may give an argument or reason to support the first line. For example:

> *Do not answer a fool according to his folly,*
> *or you will be like him yourself.* (Proverbs 26:4)

18th Bible Book

Book of Job

Faith under Trial

In the Hebrew, Greek, and Latin Bibles the eighteenth book of the Bible is called *Job*. There is some dispute over the meaning of the name. The name means either *the afflicted one* or *the penitent one*.

Job is classified as a wisdom book because it deals with a profound issue. This book explores the issue of why good people suffer. *Wisdom* is the ability to observe life from the divine point of view. *Understanding* is the ability to react to life's situations as God intends. The way we respond to our trials is directly based on our wisdom and understanding.

This book contains forty-two chapters, 1,070 verses, and 10,102 words.

Situation

The author of the Book of Job is unknown. Ancient Jewish and Christian tradition assigns the book to Moses. The time, nature, and theme of the book fit with the tradition that Moses compiled the book, possibly from records of the conversations made by Elihu (cf. 32:10-18). Many modern scholars, however, assign the book to the time of Solomon roughly a thousand years before Christ. This was a period when the writing of poetic wisdom books was flourishing in Israel.

Since the authorship of the book cannot be determined with certainty, a date cannot be assigned to the production of this book. If the authorship is ascribed to Moses, the date of writing would be about 1500 BC; if to the age of Solomon, about 950 BC. The *events* in the book seem to have taken place about 2000 BC during the Pilgrim Period. Even this, however, is not entirely certain. People in many desert regions were still living in conditions of patriarchal society even during the time of Solomon.

Job probably lived sometime between the tower of Babel episode and the death of Abram, or shortly thereafter. To tie this material to secular history, Job lived about four hundred years after the completion of the pyramids in Egypt.

Job was very wealthy (1:3, 10). He was a respected judge and benefactor of his fellow citizens (29:7-25). He was a very righteous man (1:1, 5, 8). Job was the father of seven sons and three daughters (1:2) at the outset of the story.

Plan

The Book of Job consists mostly of poetic speeches bracketed by prose narrative at beginning and end. The writer has made use of a number of poetic forms of writing such as lament, wisdom sayings, proverbs, hymns, riddles, curses, and nature poems. The poetry in this book is unsurpassed in beauty, depth, and intensity. It makes rich use of all forms of Hebrew parallelism.

Literary plan. The book is structured in a balanced pattern of threes. After the prologue (chs. 1-2) and Job's opening lament (ch. 3), there are three cycles of dialogue in which each of Job's three friends speak and are answered by Job (chs. 4-28). This is followed by three monologues, spoken by Job (chs. 29-31), Elihu (chs. 32-37), and by God (chs. 38-42). The book closes with Job's contrition and an epilogue (ch. 42).

Biographical plan. There are six main characters in the Book of Job. The basic premises of the arguments of each are summarized in the following chart.

Character	Identity	Argument
1. Satan	Adversary of God and man	Job served God for material gain
2. Job	A righteous sufferer	Accused God of injustice
3. Eliphaz	A theologian	Based argument on a vision of God
4. Bildad	A traditionalist	Based argument on time-honored concepts of justice.
5. Zophar	A dogmatist and moralist	Based argument on the consensus of human wisdom
6. Elihu	Youngest of the speakers	God refines men through suffering.

Geographical plan. The setting for the action in Job is the mysterious land of Uz. Some think Uz was in the area of Edom. Two clues suggest this: one of Job's friends comes from Teman, an Edomite city; also Edomites in ancient times were famous for their wisdom.

Eternal Purpose

The immediate purpose of the Book of Job is to provide consolation to God's people when they experience suffering in life. The ultimate purpose of the book is to show that 1) there is a benevolent divine purpose running through the suffering of the godly, and 2) that life's bitterest enigmas could be reconciled with this benevolent divine purpose if we knew all the facts.

To achieve his purpose the author shows four things. First, he shows who God really is. Second, he indicates the kind of trust God wants his children to have in him. Third, the author assures his readers that God has absolute control over Satan. Fourth, he offers some preliminary insights into the issue of why a righteous person may suffer while a wicked person prospers.

The book categorically rejects the explanation of Job's three friends that suffering is God's judgment on specific sins. Job and his critics debate, often fiercely, the reason for Job's sufferings; but each is arguing from incomplete data. Without all the factors in the equation, none can arrive at a proper solution to the problem. The text, however, is more sympathetic to the views of Elihu, the youngest speaker in the book. He asserted that suffering is God's way to teach, discipline, and refine.

By not directly answering Job's questions about suffering God is saying in the book that the issue is beyond human comprehension. Rather the believer should view suffering as a test of trust. Do we trust God unconditionally, or only if he blesses us with health and wealth? From Job we can learn that trial, suffering, and temptation test a person; they bring out the best, and the worst, in mankind. What a person is under stress, he secretly is in quiet times.

A profound truth can be learned from the silence of the book regarding a definitive explanation of suffering. There are some things which God cannot reveal to us at present, inasmuch as the very revealing of them would thwart his purposes for our good. The Scriptures contain both profound revelations and wise reservations. In them God says enough to make faith intelligent; but enough is reserved so that faith might grow and mature.

The book does not purport to give an intellectual solution to the problem of suffering. Job is more concerned with these questions: What will a truly religious person do in the face of suffering? How will suffering affect a person's relation to his God?

Dissecting this book for logical arguments will not prove rewarding. You should approach the Book of Job as a personal counselor who has learned to listen not to what people are saying, but to what they are feeling. It is in the emotional realm that estrangement from God takes place; it is there that encounter with God and reconciliation must take place as well.

The Book of Job comes to a climax in the closing speech of God. Here the Creator makes the point that if man cannot understand God's government in the natural realm, how much less can he expect to understand the principles of God's government in the spiritual realm. In respect to the issue of suffering, mankind must trust the Creator. In fact, one could even say that suffering itself is not the central theme of Job. The focus is on what Job *learns* from his suffering — the sovereignty of God over all creation. The conclusion is that God is sovereign and worthy of worship in whatever he chooses to do. Job must learn to trust in the goodness and power of God in adversity by enlarging his concept of God.

At best in this book we have an interim solution to the problem of suffering. Suffering fulfills God's purpose in this world. Through it he exercises a gracious ministry in the godly. For the believer suffering is not punitive, but remedial; not an obstacle, but an opportunity; not a penalty, but a pulpit. This is the interim solution. Someday when we no longer see through a glass darkly we will learn the final solution.

Anticipation

Job anticipates the coming of Christ both generally and specifically. The book raises a question that only Christ can answer. It expresses yearnings that only Christ can satisfy. It is full of agonizing sobs that only Christ can ease. The book points to an emptiness in the human heart that only Christ can fill. Job cries out for a Mediator (9:33; 33:23), and Christ the God/man alone can fill that office.

Like the other patriarchs, Job was a prophet. In the midst of his personal suffering he articulated two great prophecies that refer to Christ directly. First, as divine Messenger of Yahweh, Messiah will ransom men and restore their righteousness (Job 17:3). Second, Messiah the Redeemer will stand over the dust of the righteous to resurrect them (Job 19:25b).

Keys

The key chapter in the book is Job 42. In this chapter Job repents of his attitude. He no longer demands an answer as to the 'why' of his suffering.

The key verse in the book is this: *But he knows the way that I take; when he has tested me, I will come forth as gold* (Job 23:10). In this verse Job asserts his innocence of any wrongdoing deserving of the suffering he was experiencing.

The key phrase in Job is *he knows* (7).

Key words in the book include *wicked* (37), *wisdom* (23), *how?* (26) and *why?* (16).

Special Features

Here are some unusual facts about the history of the Book of Job or its content that mark this book as unique in the sacred collection:

❖ The position of Job in the Bible preceding Psalms did not become settled until the Council of Trent. This council followed the preference of the Christian scholar Jerome by fixing Job's position as the first book of the great poetic trilogy of Job, Psalms, and Proverbs.

- ❖ Job may be the oldest book of the Bible.
- ❖ Job 38–42 give the most intensive survey of creation in the Bible.
- ❖ Job depicts the earth suspended in empty space (26:7). He also implies that the earth is a sphere (22:14).
- ❖ Aunt Jemima of pancake mix fame owes her name to Job's oldest daughter in his second family (42:14).
- ❖ James 5:11 speaks of the *patience* of Job in KJV; but other versions speak of his *endurance* or *perseverance*. Actually Job was more tenacious than patient (6:8, 11).
- ❖ The book of Job contains more rare and archaic Hebrew words than any other book of the Old Testament. This makes the book one of the most difficult to translate.
- ❖ Because Job's daughters are described as the fairest in the land, a modern organization for teenage girls is called *Job's Daughters*.
- ❖ The epithet *Job's comforter* is an expression used for a person who unwittingly or maliciously depresses or discourages someone while attempting to console him.
- ❖ Several ancient stories about righteous sufferers have come to light in Mesopotamia and Egypt. Stories such as these, along with the mention of Job in other ancient Middle Eastern documents, suggest that Job and his story were widely known.
- ❖ Thomas Carlyle, the great English poet, is reputed to have said: "There is nothing written, I think, in the Bible or out of it, of equal literary merit."

HEAR

Aside from the key chapter referenced above, here are some other important chapters in the Book of Job:

- ❖ Satan on a leash (Job 1–2).
- ❖ Agony of a suffering saint (Job 3).
- ❖ Interrogation from the whirlwind (Job 38–41).

Some of the favorite lines in the Book of Job are these:

❖ *Naked I came from my mother's womb, and naked I will depart* (1:21).

❖ *I have escaped with only the skin of my teeth* (19:20).

❖ *"Skin for skin!" Satan replied. "A man will give all he has for his own life"* (2:4).

19ᵗʰ Bible Book
Book of Psalms
Faith in Various Circumstances

The Jews call the nineteenth book in our Bible *Tehillim* = *praises.* In the Greek Bible the title for this book is *Psalmoi* = *songs;* or *Psalterion (Psalter)* = *stringed instrument.* The Latin Bible fixed the name as the *Book of Psalms.*

Every part of the biblical library contributes to our relationship with God. The books of law teach. The books of history illustrate. Prophecy announces and rebukes. The epistles persuade. The Psalms, however, are designed to sweeten our relationship with the Creator. This book has shaped the prayer and worship of the saints of every age. In these pages the tested find courage; the penitent, forgiveness; the weary, rest; the downhearted, encouragement; the weeping, comfort.

Psalms has more chapters (150) than any book of the Bible. The 43,743 words are organized into 2,461 verses. This is the largest book of the Old Testament.

Situation

The individual psalms were written by at least seven different writers at various times from the days of Moses (1440 BC) to the period following the Babylonian exile. The list of contributors includes Moses (1), David (73), and Solomon (2). In addition some of the Levitical musicians of Solomon's Temple contributed psalms. These were Asaph (12), sons of Korah (10), Ethan (1), and Heman (1). Fifty of the psalms are anonymous. Many of these were probably written by David. The latest dateable Psalm is Psalm 126, which was written in the period of restoration from Babylonian captivity, ca. 525 BC. The majority of the psalms come from the time of David, ca. 1000 BC. Thus the time frame for psalm composition stretches almost a thousand years — from the exodus to the exile.

Plan

The Book of Psalms contains a variety of poetic compositions, including the following: predictive psalms (e.g., Psalms 2, 22, 45, 16, 110), praise or hallelujah psalms (e.g., 146–150), petition or supplication psalms (e.g., 6, 39, 86), penitential psalms (e.g., 32, 38, 51, 102, 130, 143), perceptive or wisdom psalms (e.g., 1, 19, 119), profession or confession psalms (e.g., 33, 107, 103), patriotic or historic psalms (e.g., 78, 105, 106), and pilgrimage psalms (e.g., 120–134).

Structural plan. The 150 individual psalms were collected into books at five different points in the history of Israel. The growth of the Book of Psalms is directly related to interest in the Temple of God. The Temple was built by Solomon ca. 959 BC. The first collection of psalms (Psalms 1–41) was written and organized by David in anticipation of the construction of the Temple. Another collection of some thirty-one psalms (Psalms 42–72) was added to the first during the religious revival in the days of good King Hezekiah about 700 BC. The third collection (Psalms 73–89) was added to the first two probably during the reformation led by King Josiah about a century after Hezekiah's revival. The fourth collection (Psalms 90–106) was added at the time the Temple was reconstructed in the days of Zerubbabel following the exile in Babylon. The final collection (Psalms 107–150) was added during the last religious revival of the Old Testament, that led by Ezra ca. 457 BC. Each collection concludes with a doxology or praise section. The following chart displays the five collections and a word about the content of each.

Structure of the Book of Psalms					
Bk	#	Doxology	Writer	Compiler	Emphasis
I	41	41:13	David	David	Adoring Worship
II	31	72:18f.	David/Korah	Hezekiah	Wondering Worship
III	17	89:52	Asaph	Josiah	Ceaseless Worship
IV	17	106:48	Anonymous	Zerubbabel	Submissive Worship
V	44	150:6	David	Ezra	Perfected Worship

Geographical plan. The psalms come from throughout the Middle East, from the Sinai desert where Moses led the Hebrews, to Israel where David built a powerful nation, to Babylon where the defeated Jews spent seventy years in exile. Thus the locale for psalm composition stretched over a thousand miles (from Egypt to Babylon).

Biographical plan. God himself is the key person of the Psalms. There can be no praise songs at all without him. Three Hebrew names of God are prominent in Psalms: *El (Elohim)* is the usual name for God. It emphasizes the power and majesty of God. *Adonay (Lord)* stresses the sovereignty of God. *Yahweh (*LORD*)* is associated with deliverance and salvation.

Eternal Purpose

The immediate purpose of the Book of Psalms is to provide for ancient Israel a worship and service hymnal. The deeper purpose was to reveal to saints of all the ages the appropriate ways to express their faith in various kinds of circumstances.

The first eighty-nine psalms focus on the human predicament. These psalms were born out of deep experiences of the soul. They include meditations, historical recitals, formal instruction, and passionate entreaty.

Beginning at Psalm 90, most of the psalms are intended for corporate worship. For good reason Psalms is sometimes called the hymnbook of Scripture. The psalms are a treasury of resources from which to draw when approaching God in prayer either as a congregation or privately. In Psalms man's soul is laid bare. Sin, sorrow, shame, repentance, hope, faith, and love are all expressed. These conditions are universal in scope, timeless in nature, and the very stuff of which prayer is made.

Psalms presents a clear-cut distinction between sin and righteousness, the wicked and the righteous.

Psalms is especially dear to every child of God, perhaps because there is no experience of the believer which does not find its counterpart in this collection. If the Bible is God's Temple of truth, Psalms is the music wing of that structure. Heavenly melody permeates this book. Here the Holy Spirit reproduces every chord of human nature from the muted, wailing note of Psalm 51, to the triumphant strains of Psalm 24.

The Book of Psalms is the mirror of the soul. It gives expression to gladness and sadness, tragedy and triumph, praise and prayer. Among the beautiful roses that compose this literary garden there are a few sharp thorns. Twelve of the psalms present special problems to Christians. In these so-called imprecatory psalms the writer calls down a curse on God's enemies. An example is Psalm 139.

In interpreting the imprecatory psalms these points need to be kept in mind: First, these psalms call for divine justice rather than human vengeance. Second, they ask for God to punish the wicked and thus vindicate his righteousness. Third, imprecatory psalms condemn sin. Fourth, even Jesus called down a curse on several cities; he told his disciples to curse cities that did not receive the gospel (Matthew 10:14-15). Fifth, most of the imprecatory psalms come from the pen of David, a man who did not have a vindictive spirit.

Anticipation

Psalms was a favorite book of the early Christians. Of the New Testament's 283 direct quotations from the Old Testament, 117 [40.3%] are from Psalms. The book contains several direct predictions of events associated with the life of Christ. This should not surprise us, since King David was considered a prophet (Acts

2:30). In the following chart the major prophecies concerning Christ in the Book of Psalms are displayed together with New Testament documentation of the fulfillment of each.

Messiah in the Book of Psalms		
Subject	Key Verses	NT Citation
1. Messiah's birth	104:4	Heb 1:7
2. Messiah's humiliation	8:4	Heb 2:6
3. Messiah's deity	45:6	Heb 1:8
4. Messiah's ministry	69:9	John 2:17
5. Messiah's rejection	118:22	Matt 21:42
6. Messiah's betrayal	41:9	John 13:18
7. Messiah's death	Ps 22	Matt 27:46
8. Messiah's resurrection	Psalms 2, 16	Acts 2:27
9. Messiah's ascension	68:18	Eph 4:8
10. Messiah's reign	102:26	Heb 1:11

Keys

The arrangement of psalms in the book is purposeful and enlightening. The book begins with an unqualified assertion that the righteous are blessed and the wicked are not (Psalm 1). In the psalms that follow this thesis is explored and sometimes questioned. Do good people always prosper and bad people always suffer? The key chapter in the Book of Psalms is Psalm 73, the first psalm of the third collection. Here the psalmist rids himself of envy of the wicked. He begins to move in the direction of the unrestrained praise of God in the closing psalms of the book.

The verse that best captures the essence of the Book of Psalms is this: *Ascribe to the* LORD *the glory due his name; worship the* LORD *in the splendor of holiness* (Psalm 29:2).

As might be expected, the key phrase in the book is *praise the* LORD/*him* (36).

Key words in Psalms are these: *The* LORD *(Yahweh)* is mentioned 536 times, in nearly one fourth of the verses. Other key words are *praise* (154), *righteous/righteousness* (131), *sin/iniquity* (67), *good* (63), *evil* (39), and *judge/judgment* (59).

Special Features

Here are some additional features related to the Book of Psalms that set it apart within the sacred collection.

- ❖ In the Hebrew Bible Psalms stands first in the third division of the books, the so-called *Kethubhim (Writings)* or *Hagiographa (Holy Writings)*. In the Greek Bible Psalms usually comes after the Book of Job as in the English Bible.

- ❖ Psalms is filled with technical terms describing the nature of the various psalms or the music that was used to accompany them. Here are a few: *Mizmor* (57 times): a song sung with musical accompaniment; *Maskil* (13 times): calls for skill or cunning; *To the chief musician* (55); *psalms of degrees* (Psalms 74–80): may have been sung by pilgrims approaching Jerusalem; or it may refer to the steps of the Temple on which the Levitical choir stood; *Selah* (71 times): thought to be a musical notation.

- ❖ Thirty-four of the psalms are called orphan psalms. They have no title of any kind.

- ❖ The shortest chapter in the Bible, and also the middle chapter, is Psalm 117. It has two verses.

- ❖ The longest chapter in the Bible is Psalm 119. It has 176 verses. It is an acrostic with eight verses beginning with each of the twenty-two letters of the Hebrew alphabet.

- ❖ The middle verse in the Bible is this one: *It is better to take refuge in the* LORD *than to trust in man* (Psalm 118:8).

- ❖ The Book of Psalms is the largest book of the Bible.

- ❖ The Book of Psalms is quoted more times in the New Testament than any other book.

- ❖ In addition to the Book of Psalms, there are at least eleven other psalms in the Old Testament. These are by Moses (Exodus 15:1-18; Deuteronomy 32:1-43), Deborah (Judges 5), Hannah (1 Samuel 2:1-10); David (2 Samuel 22:2-51), Job (chs. 3, 7, 10), Isaiah (Isaiah 12:4-6), Hezekiah (Isaiah 38:9-20), Jeremiah (Lamentations 3:19-38; ch. 5), Jonah (Jonah 2:1-9), and Habakkuk (Habakkuk 3:2-19).

- ❖ David's psalm in 2 Samuel 22:2-51 is the same as Psalm 18.

❖ There are nine acrostic psalms. The best known is Psalm 119.

HEAR

In Psalms men often speak to God in prayers of various kinds. Yet through these inspired penmen God also speaks to us. We must hear what he has to say. Here are some of the outstanding psalms with which to sample what God has for you in this book:

❖ Life's alternatives (Psalm 1).
❖ Enthronement of God's anointed (Psalm 2)
❖ The majesty of God (Psalm 8)
❖ God's two witnesses (Psalm 19)
❖ The suffering Christ (Psalm 22)
❖ Guiding Shepherd and gracious Host (Psalm 23)
❖ Approaching God's holy hill (Psalm 24)
❖ Plea of a remorseful sinner (Psalm 51)
❖ God's enduring faithfulness (Psalm 100)

Here are some favorite lines found in the Book of Psalms:

❖ *Shout for joy to the LORD all the earth* (100:1).
❖ *Your word is a lamp to my feet and a light for my path* (119:105).
❖ *The LORD is my shepherd; I shall not be in want* (23:1).
❖ *When I consider your heavens, the work of your fingers, the moon and the stars, which you have set in place, ⁴what is man that you are mindful of him, the son of man that you care for him?* (8:3-4).
❖ *As the deer pants for streams of water, so my soul pants for you, O God* (42:1).
❖ *He who dwells in the shelter of the Most High will rest in the shadow of the Almighty. ²I will say of the LORD, "He is my refuge and my fortress, my God, in whom I trust"* (91:1-2).
❖ *May the words of my mouth and the meditation of my heart be pleasing in your sight, O LORD, my Rock and my Redeemer* (19:14).

CHAPTER EIGHT

FAITH
BOOKS (2)
Proverbs–Song of Solomon

There are yet three of the Faith Books to be examined: Proverbs, Ecclesiastes, and Song of Solomon. The first two of these books are classified as wisdom books. They aim to teach. Proverbs is what scholars call prudential, i.e., practical wisdom; Ecclesiastes is what is known as philosophical wisdom. It consists of discourses on the problems of life.

Some dispute exists about how to classify the Song of Solomon. Some refer to it as wedding literature, i.e., the book is a series of love poems. It is better, however, to view Song as wisdom literature as well. It aims to explore one of the great mysteries of life, namely, the attraction of a man for a woman and vice versa.

20th Bible Book
Book of Proverbs
Faith the Foundation of Wisdom

In the Hebrew and Greek Bibles the twentieth book of the Bible is called *Proverbs of Solomon.* The Latin Bible uses a slight variation: *Book of Proverbs.*

If the Book of Psalms is designed to aid our *devotional* life, Proverbs intends to give direction for our *daily* life. The psalms speak to a right *worship*, the proverbs to a righteous *walk*. While other parts of Scripture show us the glory of our high calling in Christ, this book maps out how to *walk worthy of it*. Proverbs teaches that there is not a temper, a look, a word, a movement in the routine of daily life in which we do not either deface or adorn the image of our Lord and the profession of his name.

The book contains thirty-one chapters, 915 verses, and 15,043 words.

Situation

Solomon was the wisest man of his day. He wrote three thousand proverbs. Guided by the Holy Spirit, Solomon collected several of his proverbs into this book that was accorded a place in the sacred collection.

Solomon himself was responsible for writing major chunks of this book (1:1–22:16; chs. 25–29). Solomon was probably responsible for collecting the material in 22:17–24:34. Chapters 30–31 are of non-Israelite origin, the first being by Agur the son of Jakeh the Massaite, and the second by King Lemuel of Massa. Nothing is known about the identities of these two men. Probably it was Solomon who was guided to incorporate these two chapters into his book. King Hezekiah and his company of scribes had some role in the editing of the book (Proverbs 25:1).

The bulk of the Book of Proverbs began to take shape about 950 BC. The book may not have taken its present form prior to the time of Hezekiah, about 700 BC.

Proverbial wisdom literature is attested in Egypt and Babylonia long before the time of Solomon. The Holy Spirit directed Solomon to employ this ancient literary form to communicate divine wisdom to his people. The age of Solomon was one of peace and tranquility such as would lend itself to literary activities of this sort.

Plan

A variety of teaching techniques is employed in the Proverbs material. You will find in this book brief parables and sharp questions. You will also find an acrostic poem (31:10ff), dramatic monologue (1:20-33), and numerical sayings (30:15ff). A large portion of the book is in the form of unit proverbs ranging from one to four verses.

Literary plan. The Book of Proverbs is arranged in various collections. The first collection (1:1-9:18) is entitled *Proverbs of Solomon* (1:1). In this collection there are fifteen sonnets and two monologues. The second collection (10:1-22:16) is also entitled *Proverbs of Solomon* (10:1). In this section Solomon has gathered 375 proverbial couplets. The third (22:17-24:22) and fourth (24:23-34) collections are both entitled *Words of the Wise Men* (22:17; 24:23). The fifth collection (25:1-29:27) is entitled *Proverbs of Solomon*. This collection contains a variety of material including seven proverb clusters and fifty-five proverbial couplets. Chapters 30-31 are like an appendix to the book. These chapters contain the words of Agur and King Lemuel. In these chapters there are thirteen sayings, one discourse and one acrostic poem.

The emphasis in each of these collections can be set forth as follows:

- ❖ **Wisdom is valuable: seek it** (1:1-9:18)
- ❖ **Wisdom is practical: follow it** (10:1-22:16)
- ❖ **Wisdom is instructive: hear it** (22:17-24:34)
- ❖ **Wisdom is ethical: practice it** (chs. 30-31)

Biographical plan. While no leading characters appear in the Proverbs material, the book contains many verbal caricatures of characters we meet during life. We have all encountered *the babbling fool*, who is the expert on every subject; *the practical joker*, whose pranks more often than not end in humiliation and injury; *the gossip*, whose reckless words separate friends; *the whisperer* who shares his inside information like a chef might share a delicacy from his kitchen; *the backbiting tongue*, that smears the character of one not present; *the false boaster*, who is like wind and clouds without rain; *the get-rich-quick*, who embrace every scheme with potential to line their pockets; *the generous man*, who reaps an increase from what he scatters; *the wanderer*, who is like a restless bird; *the hermit*, who imagines that he does not need any association.

Eternal Purpose

Proverbs is one of the few biblical books that clearly spells out its purpose. See Proverbs 1:2-6. Words like *wisdom, knowledge, understanding*, and *self-discipline* are part of the teacher's agenda. The immediate purpose of the Book of Proverbs is to give Israel a handbook of wisdom. The ultimate purpose of this book is to teach that faith in God is the foundation for all wisdom and knowledge.

Community implications. Proverbs depicts society as it should be. In the society envisioned by Proverbs people work hard. They respect the rights of one another. Every person is treated with dignity. There is concern for the less fortunate. Neighbors maintain an atmosphere of general friendliness. The citizens in this ideal society avoid excesses and love their families and homes. They are sincere, modest, self-controlled, temperate, reliable, chaste, willing to listen and learn. They are forgiving, considerate, discreet, kind to animals, sweet-tempered and frugal. They are generous with others, yet not so reckless as to endanger the well-being of their own families.

Personal implications. Proverbs has a unique role in the sacred collection. Unlike the Foundation Books, Proverbs says next to nothing about worship, sacrifice, or priesthood. Unlike the twelve Framework Books, Proverbs alludes not at all to Israel's popular heroes. Unlike the prophetic books, Proverbs has nothing to say of Israel's fate, of catastrophe, or of future glory. This book says nothing about Christ's coming, immortality, Rapture, or resurrection. Proverbs is oriented to this world. This book is about prudent, moral, and practical behavior. It is a personal tune-up manual, a how-to book. The book reveals how the believer can win friends, influence people, and still please God.

Proverbs provides God's detailed instructions about how to navigate successfully through life. The book tells us how to get along with our neighbor, our spouse, our children, our boss, government bureaucrats, and even God. Much of the book is cast in the form of a father's advice to his son.

In this book Solomon aimed to place before his readers a clear-cut choice. One can choose the path of obedience or the path of rebellion, the path of industry or laziness, discipline or profligacy, and so on. Proverbs leaves no room for compromise; there is no occasion for indecision.

Basic assumptions. Everything Proverbs says must be interpreted against the backdrop of the fundamental principle of biblical wisdom: *the fear of the* LORD (reverence; faith) is the beginning of wisdom. The book assumes that the Lord is the author of morality and justice. Monotheism is presupposed.

To appreciate this book we must understand the nature of a proverb. The genius of the proverb lies in its brevity. It is a compact statement of a profound truth. It is usually worded in such a striking way that it catches on; it becomes easier to remember than to forget. A proverb does not argue; it assumes. Its purpose is not to explain a matter, but to give pointed expression to it. Furthermore a proverb states a general principle, not a guarantee from God. A great deal of harm can be done when individuals rely on individual proverbs as absolute promises of God.

The chapters of Proverbs are not meant to be read in the way one would read narratives in Kings, or full cycles of debate in Job, or complete poems as in Psalms, or the unfolding argument of Ecclesiastes. We must ponder each proverb, memorize it if possible. As a precious gem we must let the light of all of God's word reflect on its many facets.

Anticipation

There is ample evidence that Jesus loved Proverbs. Here and there in his teaching we hear an echo of its language. Here are a few examples: Jesus spoke about those who seek the chief seats (cf. Proverbs 25:6-7), the wise and foolish man and their houses (cf. Proverbs 14:11), and the rich fool (cf. Proverbs 27:1). To Nicodemus he revealed the answer to the question posed by Agur (cf. Proverbs 30:4 with John 3:13). He reminded those who, like the undiscriminating *fools* of Proverbs, do not recognize him or his message that *wisdom is justified of her children* (Matthew 11:19).

Because this book was precious to Jesus is reason enough for his disciples to study it.

There are no direct messianic predictions in Proverbs. The wisdom for which the wise man aspires, however, is embodied in Christ. He was *become for us wisdom from God* (1 Corinthians 1:30). In him are hidden *all the treasures of wisdom and knowledge* (Colossians 2:3). He exemplified without fail the ethical principles taught in Proverbs. In so doing Jesus left for us an example that we should *follow in his steps* (1 Peter 2:21).

Keys

The key chapter in Proverbs is chapter 31. In this chapter the godly wife is presented as the embodiment of the wisdom that Proverbs has been describing in the previous chapters. The key verse of the book is this: *The fear of the LORD is the beginning of knowledge* (Proverbs 1:7). This thought is repeated in a slightly different form in 9:10. The concluding verses of the book attribute this fear of the Lord to the godly wife (31:30). Appearing as it does at the beginning and end as well as within the body of the book clearly indicates that everything within this book must be interpreted in the light of the principle of godly fear (reverence).

Key phrases in Proverbs are *my son* (23) and *fear of the LORD* (14).

The key words include *but* (243), *righteous* (54), *wisdom* (53), *evil* (50), *knowledge* (42), *life* (38) and *instruction* (25). Wisdom is the ability to live life skillfully, i.e., live a godly life in an ungodly world.

Special Features

Some features that distinguish Proverbs in the sacred collection are these:

- ❖ Proverbs has a nine-chapter introduction—a lengthy essay contrasting wisdom with foolishness.
- ❖ Proverbs ends with an acrostic poem praising a good wife. She is the counterpart of Lady Wisdom who is described in the early chapters of the book.
- ❖ Although Solomon wrote three thousand proverbs (1 Kings 4:32), only about eight hundred have survived in the Book of Proverbs.

❖ There are at least fourteen New Testament quotations or allusions to Proverbs.

HEAR

The biblical proverbs are not merely tersely expressed deductions from daily experience of a worldly-wise man. They are also divine precepts (whether expressed or implied). Moreover, the biblical proverbs point to the fear of the Lord as the basic principle of all true knowledge. We devalue the book when we fail to hear God's voice in it. Some favorite lines in Proverbs are these:

❖ *He who spares the rod hates his son* (13:24).
❖ *Pride goes before destruction* (16:18).
❖ *Trust in the* LORD *with all your heart and lean not on your own understanding* (3:5).
❖ *Train a child in the way he should go: and when he is old, he will not turn from it* (22:6).
❖ *A gentle answer turns away wrath* (15:1).

21st Bible Book
Book of Ecclesiastes
Faith the Key to Meaning

In Jewish tradition the twenty-first book in our Bible is called *Qohelet* or *Koheleth*. This is the word that is translated *Preacher* or *Teacher* in 1:1. It means literally *one who assembles*. Our English name *Ecclesiastes* is derived from the Greek and Latin Bibles. This term in Greek refers to *one who addresses the assembly of citizens.*

The book contains twelve chapters, 222 verses, and 5,584 words.

Situation

Jewish tradition from the earliest times attributed Ecclesiastes to Solomon, although there is some suggestion in the tradition that King Hezekiah's scribes may have edited the text. Circumstantial evidence within the text supports the conclusion of Jewish tradition. The author was *son of David and king in Jerusalem*. He was wise, rich, had many wives, and engaged in numerous public works. In spite of the rather clear-cut evidence that Solomon is author, many conservative scholars take the position that the book is anonymous.

Some suggest that Solomon wrote Song of Songs in his youth, Proverbs in his maturity, and Ecclesiastes toward the end of his reign of forty years (935 BC). In spite of the great prosperity that characterized Solomon's reign, the people were gradually drifting away from the Lord. Solomon could see evil days ahead for his people because of their apostasy which he himself had to some degree encouraged. Ecclesiastes is the evidence of the personal repentance of Solomon; it is also an exhortation to his subjects to reassess the meaning of their lives.

Plan

Ecclesiastes contains a variety of forms of literature including general reflections (1:2-11; 3:1-8; 7:1-8 etc.), personal (first person) reflections (1:12-18; 2:1-13), exhortations (4:17–5:8; 7:9-14; 11:1-6; etc.), and individual wisdom sayings (9:17–10:20).

The Book of Ecclesiastes is structured like a sermon. There is the announcement of a theme, a brief introduction, a developing of the theme, and a practical application in conclusion.

The theme of Ecclesiastes is *the quest for the supreme good*.

The book begins with an introduction in which Solomon sets forth his subject (1:1-11). He then describes his quest. First, he describes the results of his personal investigation (1:12–2:26). Here he identifies several blind alleys he went down in search of the supreme good — wine, women, work, worldly wisdom — all of which he found to be meaningless endeavors. Second, Solomon continued the quest by noting things he had observed in life — meaningless times and conditions (chs. 3–6). Third, Solomon continued the quest by practical morality (chs. 7–10). He speaks in this section of things he had studied — wisdom amidst wickedness, purpose amidst perplexities. Fourth, the quest for the supreme good concludes with an appeal for worship from the womb to the tomb (chs. 11–12). This is the supreme good in life.

Eternal Purpose

The immediate purpose of Ecclesiastes is to testify to Solomon's personal reassessment of life's priorities. Ecclesiastes is an inspired confession of failure and pessimism coming from the lips of a man who wasted most of his life. The writer calls upon his countrymen to make the same reassessment. An anonymous writer has written: "Ecclesiastes is the sphinx of Hebrew literature with its unsolved riddles of history and life." The ultimate purpose of the book is to demonstrate that faith is the key to meaning in life.

Key points. The book stresses two key points, which are in reality the flip side of each other. First, no true happiness is found in what this world has to offer. Second, true satisfaction is found only in God. As was the case with Proverbs, the underlying premise of the book is that the fear of God is the beginning of wisdom.

Ecclesiastes presents clear truths about God and man: God's existence (3:14; 5:2), God's sovereignty and power (6:2; 7:13; 9:1), God's justice (5:8; 8:12-13), man's sinfulness (7:20; 9:3), man's finiteness (8:8, 17), man's duty (9:7-10; 12:13), man's immortality (3:11; 12:7), and divine punishment and rewards (2:26; 3:17; 8:12; 11:9; 12:14).

Perhaps the most valuable lesson to be learned from this book is that death is inescapable. The shadow of death falls on everything we do. It is the *fly in the ointment* (10:1) of all that the worldly man accomplishes. Ecclesiastes forcefully exposes the bankruptcy of materialistic and non-Christian philosophies of life.

Alternating perspectives. Solomon's strategy in the book is to place in contrast two very different views of life. First, he views things around him as the natural man would do, without the light of divine revelation. He signals this view when he uses the phrase *under the sun* twenty-nine times in the book. In some sections of the book Solomon relies only on the power of human reason. He states seven times that he *communed with his own heart*. Solomon's conclusion is that apart from God *all is vanity* (emptiness). Nothing this world offers can fill the God-shaped void in man's life but God himself!

In contrast with this view of earthly emptiness, Solomon views life from the perspective of a believer. Now his conclusions have the ring of certainty and hope. This pattern of alternating perspectives continues throughout the book.

The writer hints of his methodology in 12:11. There he speaks of two types of wisdom material: the *goads* and the *nails*. The *goads* are probing issues that make people think; they are problems to be solved. The *nails* are the solutions, principles upon which the seeker can hang his faith. The following chart displays some of these problems and solutions.

Goads: Problems to Ponder	Nails: Suggested Solutions
1st Goad: Striving after earthly wisdom and selfish pursuits is unsatisfying (1:1–2:23).	1st Nail: Gratefully accept the good gifts from God's hand (2:24-26). 2nd Nail: Life is God's gift; it must be viewed in the light of eternity (3:1-15).
2nd Goad: The same fate awaits both humans and animals (3:16–4:16).	3rd Nail: The highest good should be sought at the house of God and by obeying his ordinances (5:1-20).
3rd Goad: Who knows what is good for man in life? (6:1-12).	4th Nail: Wisdom is as good as an inheritance (7:1-29).
4th Goad: Who is the wise man? (8:1)	5th Nail: The wise man's heart discerns time and judgment (8:2-5).
5th Goad: Man's misery is great upon him (8:6-8).	6th Nail: It shall be well with them that fear God (8:9-13).
6th Goad: The righteous experience the same fate as the wicked (8:14-15).	7th Nail: The righteous and their works are in the hands of God (8:16–9:1).
7th Goad: All things come alike to him that sacrifices and him that that does not sacrifice (9:2-6).	8th Nail: God has already accepted your works, let your garments be always white (9:7-10).

Personal obligation. Some accuse Ecclesiastes of teaching Epicureanism — eat, drink for tomorrow we shall die. Actually the book provides a counterbalance to those who view biblical faith as stern, pale, and joyless. It is good that at least one book of the sacred collection reminds us that we have a duty to enjoy life. We express our gratitude to the Lord by enjoying the manifold beauties and blessings of the wonderful life he has bestowed upon us.

Anticipation

There are no direct prophecies of the coming of Messiah in Ecclesiastes. Yet the shadow of Christ falls across the pages of this book. Christ is the supreme good, the ultimate satisfaction for which the believer aspires (cf. John 4:13-14). Christ also is the *one Shepherd* or teacher from whom the wisdom of this book comes (12:11; cf. John 10:1; Colossians 2:3). Christ is both the Water of Life and the Wisdom of God. As the former he quenches our thirst for happiness; as the latter he satisfies our desire to understand the true meaning of life.

Keys

The key chapter in Ecclesiastes is chapter 12. In this chapter Solomon comes to his grand conclusion that only in serving God is there any meaning in life. Within that chapter the key verse is this: *Let us hear the conclusion of the whole matter: Fear God, and keep his commandments: for this is the whole duty of man* (12:13).

The key phrases in the book are *under the sun* (29) and *vexation of spirit* (9).

Key words in Ecclesiastes include *God* (42), *vanity* (33), *wisdom* (28), and *evil* (21).

Special Features

Here are some facts about Ecclesiastes that make it unique in the Bible.

❖ In the Hebrew Bible this book is grouped with Ruth, Song of Solomon, Lamentations, and Esther as part of the *Megilloth* (*Scrolls*). These five books were read at various solemn assemblies during the year by the Jews.

❖ In the Greek Bible the three books attributed to Solomon (Proverbs, Ecclesiastes, Song of Solomon) follow Psalms, which was attributed to Solomon's father

David. The English arrangement of books has followed that of the Greek Old Testament.

❖ Ecclesiastes is the most philosophical book of the Bible.

❖ In rabbinic circles there was an ongoing debate about whether this book belonged in the sacred canon. The greatest rabbis, however, defended the right of the book to be in the Bible.

❖ The writer uses exclusively *Elohim* for God rather than LORD (*Yahweh*). He has in mind the Creator/creature relationship rather than the Redeemer/redeemed relationship.

HEAR

Three basic approaches to Ecclesiastes are represented in the literature. First, the purely naturalistic approach rejects Ecclesiastes because it allegedly teaches a fatalistic (7:13), pessimistic (4:2), materialistic (3:19-21), hedonistic (2:24), agnostic (1:13) view of life. Second, the partially theistic approach regards everything from 1:3-12:12 as a record of what a natural man thinks about life. The only positive word of God is found in 12:13-14. The third and correct view is that the book is entirely theistic, i.e., it was written by a person of faith for people of faith. Once one understands the writer's methodology (outlined above) the entire book is true, but not necessarily the whole truth.

The message of Ecclesiastes often has been misunderstood. Pessimists find verses here to bolster their dreary views of life. Skeptics claim support from this book for their contention that man does not survive death. Members of cults like the Jehovah's Witnesses quote Ecclesiastes to confirm their theory of soul-sleeping between the death of the body and the yet-future resurrection. In addition a host of sincere believers have become confused by what appear to be unspiritual dictums in the book, which they view as contradictory to the principles of the New Testament. Yet this is a book God intends for us to read, but read with discernment. Before undertaking a study of Ecclesiastes, please review the section on Eternal Purpose above.

Here are a few of the favorite lines from this book:

❖ *Eat and drink and be glad* (8:15).

❖ *There is a time for everything, and a season for every activity under heaven* (3:1).

❖ *Cast your bread upon the waters* (11:1).

❖ *There is nothing new under the sun* (1:9).

❖ *Remember your Creator in the days of your youth* (12:1).

❖ *Of making many books there is no end; and much study wearies the body* (12:12).

❖ *Utterly meaningless! Everything is meaningless* (1:2).

❖ *A man can do nothing better than to eat and drink and find satisfaction in his work. This too, I see, is from the hand of God, for without him, who can eat or find enjoyment?* (2:24-25).

Here is a suggestion that might make your reading of Ecclesiastes more fruitful. Construct a chart in two columns. Label the left column: "Life under the Sun." Deduce from the following references what life *under the sun* (without God) is like: 1:3; 1:9; 1:14; 2:18; 6:12; 8:15; 8:17; 9:3; 9:11; 12:2. Label column two "Life under the Son." Analyze the following New Testament references that seem to give a point-by-point rebuttal to the rather gloomy conclusions of Ecclesiastes: Philippians 1:6; 2 Corinthians 5:17; 1 Corinthians 15:58; Colossians 1:10; John 3:16; Philippians 2:13; 1 Corinthians 13:12; 1 John 5:11; 1 Corinthians 1:27; 1 John 5:13. Feel free to use a substitute New Testament Scripture if you can think of a better one in each case. When your assignment is complete you should have two columns contrasting a life without hope on the left, with the life of hope in Christ on the right.

22ⁿᵈ Bible Book

Song of Songs
Faith Expressed in Love

In Jewish tradition the twenty-second book of our Bible is called: *Song of Songs*. This title is derived from the first verse. The Greek and Latin Bibles took the same name. The name *Canticles*, which is used for this book in some Catholic versions, is derived from the Latin Bible. How appropriate it is that this book, which deals with the theme of themes — love — is called the Song of Songs.

Song of Solomon contains eight chapters, 117 verses, and 2,661 words.

To turn from the gloom of Ecclesiastes to the exhilaration of the Song of Solomon is like stepping out of the wilderness into the Promised Land, like the bright shining of the sun after a storm. One can maintain a healthy balance in Bible study by studying these books back to back. Ecclesiastes focuses on the *intellect* of man — his mental outlook on life. The Song of Solomon speaks about the emotions of man — in particular, the *emotion* of love. Both the head and heart of the believer must be in subjection to the Lord.

Situation

The opening verse attributes the Song to Solomon. Internal and external evidence supports this claim. The book was probably written about 965 BC.

Solomon ascended the throne in 971 BC. He is famous among other things, for his many wives and concubines (1 Kings 11:3). Most of these marriages were political alliances. On a trip to the northern part of his land, Solomon met and fell in love with a beautiful maiden. She was given by her brothers in marriage to the king. The Shulamite maiden, however, loved a shepherd back in her area. The book depicts in poetic verse Solomon's attempt to woo this maiden to true love, and her steadfast determination to remain faithful to her beloved.

Plan

The Song consists entirely of poetic dialogue. The problem is that the writer seldom has identified the speakers. No two analyses of the book identify the speakers in the same way. The NIV gives some helpful direction on this matter; but even in the Hebrew text it is not always clear who is doing the speaking.

At least six voices are heard in the book: In chapters 1–7 there is interchange between Solomon's harem, the Shulamite maiden, and Solomon himself. The narrator speaks in 3:6-11 and 8:5a. In chapter 8 two new voices are heard, that of the shepherd (8:5b, 13) and the Shulamite's brothers (8:8-9).

Like Ecclesiastes, this little book is not easily outlined. The dramatic reading seems to have four acts, the first three of which are set in or about Solomon's Jerusalem palace. In these three acts the Shulamite's love for her shepherd is besieged by Solomon's flattery and gifts. The maiden's love is fortified with fantasies of the days of courtship with her beloved. This alternating pattern of love besieged and love fortified can be seen in the following breakdown:

> Act One: Initial Assault (1:2-3:5)
> > A. Love besieged (1:2-2:7)
> > B. Love fortified (2:8-3:5)
> Act Two: Intensified Assault (3:6-6:3)
> > A. Love besieged (3:6-5:1)
> > B. Love fortified (5:2-6:3)
> Act Three: Final Assault (6:4-8:4)
> > A. Love besieged (6:4-7:9)
> > B. Love fortified (7:10-8:4)

The setting for Act Four (8:5-14) is in a garden back in the home area of the Shulamite. The Shulamite has been reunited with her beloved shepherd. True love has triumphed.

Not everyone agrees with this analysis of the Song. The more popular view is that the romantic dialogue is an exchange between Solomon and the Shulamite on the eve of their wedding. The crux issue over which scholars disagree is whether the shepherd referenced in the book is a figurative title for Solomon. Even allowing for poetic license, it is hard to imagine the great King Solomon behaving in ways even remotely similar to the ways that the Shulamite attributes to her shepherd. If the shepherd is not Solomon, then one must assume that the maiden is recalling past courtship as a means of dealing with the wooing of the king who always got his woman.

Eternal Purpose

The Song of Songs has always been controversial. There is no book of Scripture on which more commentaries have been written and more diversity of opinion expressed than this short dramatic poem of eight chapters.

The immediate purpose of the Song is to bear testimony to, and thereby applaud, the steadfast loyalty of one maiden for her beloved. The deeper purpose of the book is to describe and put God's seal of approval upon romantic love. No other book of the Bible gives such an extended description of the beauties of a love relationship between a man and a woman.

Committed love is a proper concern of religion. Rightly harnessed in marriage the mutual attraction of a man and a woman is like a raging river made productive through dams and locks. Unharnessed this mighty force is like a rampaging river in flood—dealing death and destruction. Too long love and marriage have been the private preserve of disc jockeys, Hollywood cinema, and Madison Avenue sales pitches. Physical love—dare we say sexual love—is the deep responsibility of the church.

Anticipation

There is no specific messianic prophecy in the Song. In Ephesians 5:28-33 Paul seems to say that love is a mystery that foreshadows the love of Christ for his bride the church. The capacity to appreciate the intimacy of marital love may be a stepping-stone to help us grasp our heavenly union with Christ. Christians should love their Lord with the same intensity and loyalty as the Shulamite loved her shepherd.

Keys

The key chapter in the Song of Songs is chapter 8. In this chapter the Shulamite maiden is reunited with her beloved. She then serves as an example of virtue to her younger sister.

The key verse in the book is this: *I am my lover's, and my lover is mine* (6:3a). This verse occurs again in slight variation in 2:16.

The key phrase in Song is *daughters of Jerusalem* (10).

Key words include *beloved* (30), *love* (26), and *fair* (11).

Special Features

Some of the special features that set Song apart in the sacred collection are these:

❖ In the Hebrew Bible Song is included along with Ruth, Esther, Lamentations, and Ecclesiastes as one of the *Megilloth* (scrolls) because it was read annually at the Passover feast. The position of the book in the English Bible is taken from the Greek Old Testament.

❖ Like the book of Esther, the Song of Songs does not mention God.

❖ Of the 1,005 songs that Solomon wrote (1 Kings 4:32), this is the only one that has survived.

❖ Among the rabbis the right of this book to have a place in the Bible was debated. The greatest of the rabbis came out in favor of its inclusion.

❖ In love songs from the ancient world the lovers refer to one another as *brother* and *sister* just as in the Song of Songs.

❖ Some interpreters feel uncomfortable treating this book as a love song about a man and a woman. They developed symbolic ways of looking at the book. Some Jews took the man to represent God, and the woman, Israel. For the early Christians, the man was Christ, and the bride, the church.

❖ This love song refers to twenty-one species of plants and fifteen species of animals.

❖ Because of its poetic imagery the Song uses forty-nine words that occur nowhere else in Scripture.

HEAR

The Song comes as a shock to those who have hang-ups about romantic love. Many believers through the ages have recoiled at the frank and intimate expressions of love in this book. The Song, however, sounds the death knell to the two major perversions of the holiness of marriage—asceticism and lust. Those who are aroused licentiously by reading this book are out of tune with its purpose. Those who are embarrassed by reading this book do not see the purity and true beauty of marital love.

Aside from the key verse, here is another famous line from this book: *I am a rose of Sharon, a lily of the valleys* (2:1).

CHAPTER NINE

FOCUS BOOKS (1)
Isaiah–Lamentations

There are two shelves of Focus Books in the Old Testament library. The first shelf contains four large books and one that is very small. Two of these books come from the period prior to Israel's exile to Babylon, and two after. A small book focusing on the destruction of Jerusalem in 586 BC serves as a connecting link between the two sets. Because of their size these books are called Major Prophets.

Larger Focus Books		
Isaiah	Lamentations	Ezekiel
Jeremiah	*Connecting link*	Daniel

The second shelf contains a series of twelve small books, nine of which come from the period before Israel's exile to Babylon. Chronologically, four of these books — Joel, Amos, Obadiah, Jonah — come from before the time of Isaiah. Two — Hosea, Micah — are contemporary with Isaiah. Two — Nahum, Zephaniah — come from the period between Isaiah and Jeremiah. One — Habakkuk — is contemporary with Jeremiah. The remaining three books on this shelf date to the time after Israel's return from Babylon. Because of their size these books are called Minor Prophets. In the Hebrew tradition these twelve separate books were counted as one book called *The Twelve*.

Smaller Focus Books			
Hosea	Obadiah	Nahum	Haggai
Joel	Jonah	Habakkuk	Zechariah
Amos	Micah	Zephaniah	Malachi

The sixteen contributors to the Focus shelves appeared on the stage of Israel's history in roughly this order: Obadiah (845 BC), Joel (835 BC), Jonah (755 BC), Amos (755 BC), Hosea (752 BC), Isaiah (739 BC), Micah (735 BC), Nahum (654 BC), Zephaniah (630 BC), Jeremiah (627 BC), Habakkuk (609 BC), Daniel (604 BC), Ezekiel (593 BC), Haggai (520 BC), Zechariah (520 BC), and Malachi (432 BC).

For the most part the Focus Books contain three kinds of material: sermons rebuking current sin, warnings of impending judgment, and promises of better things to come.

23rd Bible Book
Book of Isaiah
The Gospel Prophet

The twenty-third book of the Bible is named after the author. The name *Isaiah* means *Yahweh is salvation*. This essentially is the same meaning as the name *Joshua*. Isaiah has been called *the Prince of the Old Testament Prophets* (Copass), *the Saint Paul of the Old Testament* (Robinson), and *the greatest prophet* (Eusebius). This man was a theologian, reformer, statesman, historian, poet, orator, prince, and patriot.

The Book of Isaiah has been called *the Mount Everest of prophetic literature*. The intrinsic grandeur of this book attracts those who are connoisseurs of great literature. Students of theology find here sublime revelations of God's character. The evangelical emphasis of the book has made it a favorite of Christian preachers through the ages. Those who defend biblical revelation find in these prophecies abundant evidence of supernatural revelation. Simple believers rejoice in a treasure trove of passages which encourage them in their Christian pilgrimage.

Isaiah was the son of a man named Amoz. He served as court historian during the reigns of Jotham and Hezekiah (2 Chronicles 26:22; 32:32). Isaiah was married. His wife is called *the prophetess*. He had at least two sons who were given the symbolic names *Shear-jashub* (7:3) and *Maher-shalal-hash-baz* (8:1). The former name means, *a remnant shall return*; the latter, *quick to the plunder, swift to the spoil*. Isaiah was a resident of the city of Jerusalem.

Isaiah was called to the prophetic ministry in the year that King Uzziah died, 740 BC. The exact termination point of his ministry cannot be determined with certainty. Jewish tradition says he died by being sawn asunder by wicked King Manasseh. A date of about 685 BC for his death would not be far off.

The Book of Isaiah has sixty-six chapters, 1,292 verses, and 37,044 words. It is the fourth largest book in the Old Testament.

Situation

Isaiah rightly has been called *the great central prophet*. His ministry was central in time. He walked across the stage of history roughly halfway between Moses and Christ. Isaiah was central in the events of history. He lived during the days of the mighty Assyrian Empire. He anticipated the downfall of that empire and the rise of its two successors, the Chaldean and the Persian empires. This prophet was central in theological emphasis. He drove home the great principles of salvation through faith, substitutionary atonement, the kingdom, and resurrection. Isaiah was also central among the prophetic books.

Isaiah's ministry centers around two crises in the history of Judah. First, in 734 BC Judah was invaded by the king of Israel and his ally the king of Damascus. Their intent was to remove Ahaz, the rightful king, and replace him with a man more inclined to join them in resisting Assyria. Isaiah offered Ahaz encouragement during this crisis (Isaiah 7). Ahaz, however, chose to negotiate for assistance from the Assyrians rather than follow the path of trust advocated by Isaiah.

The second crisis was even more serious. In 701 BC Judah was invaded by a massive Assyrian army led by King Sennacherib.

The Assyrians quickly conquered all the outlying villages of Judah. Judean King Hezekiah holed up behind Jerusalem's walls. Isaiah assured him that the Assyrians would not fire one arrow against Jerusalem. That night the angel of God passed through the Assyrian camp. He smote 185,000 Assyrian soldiers. Sennacherib was forced to make a hasty withdrawal with what was left of his army.

The prophet Micah was a contemporary of Isaiah in Judah. The long ministry of Hosea in the northern kingdom probably overlapped that of Isaiah in the south.

There are four key dates in the ministry of Isaiah:

- ❖ 740 BC   Isaiah's call to ministry
- ❖ 734 BC   Judah invaded by hostile coalition
- ❖ 723 BC   Israel destroyed by Assyrians
- ❖ 701 BC   Assyrian invasion of Judah

Plan

The Book of Isaiah consists mostly of prophetic oracles and sermons. There are also some songs in the book, and a four-chapter section of historical narrative.

The book contains 111 separate predictions. Of the 1,292 verses in the book, 754 (59%) deal with future events. Isaiah saw more of the future of salvation than any other Old Testament prophet.

Structural plan. The Book of Isaiah is organized into two major divisions of thirty-five chapters and twenty-seven chapters respectively. These two blocks of material are joined together by a narrative section. The structure of the book is displayed in the following chart.

Structure of the Book of Isaiah			
Mostly Threats of Judgment	Historical Connecting Link		Mostly Promises of Deliverance
Chs. 1–35	Chs. 36–37	Chs. 38–39	Chs. 40–66
Coming of Assyrians Anticipated	Assyrian Attack	Coming of Babylonians Anticipated	Babylonian Conquest Assumed

Biographical plan. There are three major characters in the book besides Isaiah himself. **Ahaz** was the wicked king of Judah who rejected Isaiah's offer of a sign in the crisis of 734 BC. **Hezekiah** was the good king of Judah who was ruling when the Assyrians overran the country and nearly destroyed Jerusalem. **Cyrus** was the Persian king who was named by Isaiah as the deliverer of Jews deported to Babylon.

Geographical plan. The main focus of Isaiah is the kingdom of Judah. In addition the prophet makes pronouncements about several Gentile nations from Cush (Ethiopia) in the south to Babylon and Elam in the east.

Eternal Purpose

The immediate purpose of the Book of Isaiah is to teach the truth that salvation is by grace through faith. The deeper purpose of the book is to show Judah as a messianic nation and the channel through which the Messiah was to enter the world.

The book is rich in theology. Isaiah's distinctive title for God, *the Holy One of Israel*, emphasizes both God's apartness from the world and his solidarity with his people. Isaiah presents Yahweh as Creator, King, and Savior of Israel. He is *the Mighty God* who sends forth his Servant (Messiah) to die for the sins of mankind.

Anticipation

For the Christian the Book of Isaiah is extremely important. Forty-seven chapters of this book were directly quoted or alluded to by Christ or the apostles. With more than four hundred allusions, Isaiah stands second only to Psalms as the most cited book in the New Testament.

Isaiah's vision of the Savior is the most moving as well as the clearest of all Old Testament portraits. His many prophecies of Christ make Isaiah the prophet of the gospel before the gospel. He might well be called the fifth evangelist. There are at least seventeen passages in the book (119 verses) that pertain directly to Christ. Isaiah foresaw the whole range of Christ's life:

❖ His birth (7:14; 9:6)
❖ His family (11:1)
❖ His anointing (11:2)
❖ His character (11:3-4)
❖ His gentleness (42:1-2)
❖ His preaching (61:1-11)
❖ His death (ch. 53)
❖ His resurrection (53:10; 25:8)
❖ His glorious kingdom (2:1-4; 65:17-25)

Keys

The key chapters in Isaiah are chapters 36–39. These chapters tie together the entire book. Chapters 36–37 relate the fulfillment of all that Isaiah had been saying for almost four decades. Chapters 38–39 anticipate the deportation to Babylon that is assumed to have taken place in the last twenty-seven chapters of the book.

The key verse is this: *See, I lay a stone in Zion, a tested stone, a precious cornerstone for a sure foundation; the one who trusts will never be dismayed* (Isaiah 28:16). This verse captures twin points of emphasis in the book, namely, the coming of Messiah and the principle of trust.

The key phrase in Isaiah is his favorite name for God: *Holy One of Israel* (25).

Key words include *Zion* (46), *salvation* (28), *trust* (17), and *save/saved* (19).

Special Features

Here are some facts that distinguish Isaiah within the biblical library:

❖ The longest word in the Bible is the name of Isaiah's son: *Maher-shalal-hash-baz* (8:1).
❖ Isaiah is like a miniature Bible. It breaks into two main divisions of thirty-nine chapters of judgment followed by twenty-seven chapters of comfort. Coincidentally the Bible also breaks into two main sections of thirty-

nine books (the Old Testament) followed by twenty-seven books (the New Testament).

❖ Isaiah walked barefoot and "naked" (minus his outer garment) for three years to forecast the fate of Egypt and to warn Judah not to join the Egyptians in a rebellion against Assyria (20:1-6).

❖ Isaiah named Cyrus — the Persian king who came along two hundred years later — as the leader who would permit the Jews to return from Babylon (44:28; 45:1).

HEAR

Here is a sampling of outstanding chapters in the Book of Isaiah:

❖ Isaiah's call (Isaiah 6)
❖ A peaceful kingdom (Isaiah 11)
❖ A word of comfort (Isaiah 40)
❖ God's great deliverance (Isaiah 40–48)
❖ The futility of idolatry (Isaiah 44)
❖ The suffering servant (Isaiah 53)
❖ The world to come (65:17-25)

There are so many favorite verses in Isaiah that it is hard to select only a few for this introduction. Perhaps you can add to this list of favorites.

❖ *They shall beat their swords into plowshares and their spears into pruning hooks. Nation will not take up sword against nation, nor will they train for war anymore* (2:4b).

❖ *I heard the voice of the* LORD *saying, "Whom shall I send? And who will go for us?" And I said, "Here am I. Send me!"* (6:8).

❖ *"Come now, let us reason together," says the* LORD. *"Though your sins are like scarlet, they shall be as white as snow; though they are red as crimson, they shall be like wool"* (1:18).

❖ *The grass withers and the flowers fall, but the word of our God stands forever* (40:8).

❖ *Those who hope in the* LORD *will renew their strength. They will soar on wings like eagles; they will run and not grow weary, they will walk and not be faint* (40:31).

❖ *Come, all you who are thirsty,, come to the waters; and you who have no money, come, buy and eat. Come, buy wine and milk without money and without cost* (55:1).

24ᵗʰ Bible Book

Book of Jeremiah
The Weeping Prophet

The twenty-fourth book of the Bible is named after its author and hero. The name *Jeremiah* means something like *whom Yahweh appoints* or *whom Yahweh throws*. Seven other men in the Bible have this name. This Jeremiah was the son of Hilkiah the priest (1:1), possibly the famous high priest of this period (2 Kings 22:4). Jeremiah came from the village of Anathoth within eyesight of the northern wall of Jerusalem.

Jeremiah has been called the *Weeping Prophet*, the *Martyr Prophet*, and *God's Iron Pillar*. He is one of the more interesting prophets simply because so much is known about his life. His biography is a living sermon, and his book is a mini Bible. Saints throughout the ages have been challenged and inspired by Jeremiah's deeds and words.

The Book of Jeremiah contains fifty-two chapters, 1,364 verses, and 42,659 words. By word count, this is the longest of the prophetic books and second in size only to the Book of Psalms in the Old Testament.

Situation

Jeremiah began to prophesy in the midst of the last great revival of Judah under King Josiah. That revival effort reached its climax in 621 BC with the discovery of the lost law book in the Temple. After Josiah was killed in battle at Megiddo by Pharaoh Neco (609 BC), the political situation deteriorated rapidly in Judah. Pharaoh put Josiah's son Jehoiakim on the throne of Judah. This king hated Jeremiah and attempted on more than one occasion to kill him.

During the reign of Jehoiakim the balance of power shifted in the Middle East. In the Battle of Carchemish (605 BC) Nebuchadnezzar defeated Pharaoh Neco and became master of the region. Jehoiakim sent hostages to Babylon in 605–604 BC as proof of his willingness to serve the Babylonian. Among those captives was Daniel.

Jehoiakim rebelled against Nebuchadnezzar, but died before the Babylonian could punish him. His son with the sound-alike name *Jehoiachin* surrendered Jerusalem to Nebuchadnezzar in 597 BC. Ten thousand Jews were deported including the king and Ezekiel. Nebuchadnezzar appointed the last king of Judah, *Zedekiah*. After eleven years of rule, Zedekiah also rebelled. This time the Babylonians came and totally destroyed Jerusalem.

Jeremiah was called to preach as a teenager (Jeremiah 1). The year was 627 BC, the thirteenth year of King Josiah. Jeremiah's ministry was colorful to say the least. He not only preached dramatically, he performed a number of action parables in which he acted out the main point of his message. Jeremiah's ministry was painful as well. He experienced horrendous persecution. He also lived through the agony of the fall of Jerusalem to the Babylonians.

The ministry of this prophet extended to about 575 BC—a ministry of about fifty-two years. Other prophets who were on the scene during this same period were Habakkuk, Daniel, and Ezekiel.

Here are the key dates during Jeremiah's ministry:

- ❖ Jeremiah's call   627 BC
- ❖ Lost law scroll found   621 BC
- ❖ Battle of Carchemish   605 BC
- ❖ Deportation of 10,000 Jews   597 BC
- ❖ Jerusalem destroyed   586 BC

Plan

The Book of Jeremiah is a collection of sermons preached over five decades. These sermons are interspersed with powerful poetic oracles, prayers, narratives, and emotional reactions to events.

The sensitive prophet from Anathoth was perplexed and devastated by the hostile reception he received from his countrymen.

The arrangement of materials in the Book of Jeremiah has been called the most confused in the Old Testament. Large blocks of the material are in chronological order. Here and there, however, chapters are inserted which jump forward or backward in time. Jeremiah or his editor Baruch must have grouped material at times according to a topical rather than a chronological principle.

Structural plan. The first chapter of Jeremiah serves as an introduction to the book. It relates the call of Jeremiah to prophetic ministry. The remaining chapters fall into two large divisions: the *words* of Jeremiah (chs. 2-25) and the *life* of Jeremiah (chs. 26-51). Chapter 52 is an appendix, probably added by Jeremiah's scribe Baruch, documenting the fulfillment of Jeremiah's controversial prophecy concerning the destruction of Jerusalem.

The first major division — the words — consists of public pronouncements (chs. 2-10), private discouragement (chs. 11-26), and messages about political corruption (chs. 21-25).

The second major division — the life — consists of Jeremiah's suffering (chs. 26-29), Judah prophecies (chs. 30-35), more of Jeremiah's suffering (chs. 36-45), and Gentile prophecies (chs. 46-51). The Battle of Carchemish (605 BC) marks the division between the two major divisions of the book.

Biographical plan. The leading characters of the book are the following: Jeremiah and his scribe **Baruch**. Two Judean kings, **Jehoiakim** and **Zedekiah**, also play a prominent role. Jeremiah faced two powerful enemies during his ministry: **Pashur** (a priest) and **Hananiah** (a false prophet). Finally, the shadow of the great king **Nebuchadnezzar** falls across much of Jeremiah's message.

Geographical plan. The Book of Jeremiah embraces the entire Near East. Jeremiah himself ministered mostly in Jerusalem. His last years, however, were spent in Egypt. Jeremiah spoke a great deal about Babylon. He once wrote a letter to the Jewish captives in that place.

Eternal Purpose

The immediate purpose of Jeremiah is to induce the citizens of Judah to submit themselves to the authority of God and the yoke of Babylon. The deeper purpose of the book is to encourage faithfulness in ministry in the midst of the most difficult circumstances.

Jeremiah stressed the sovereignty of God. The Lord had decreed that all the nations must serve the king of Babylon for seventy years (25:11). Judah's repentance should manifest itself in submission to Nebuchadnezzar. Otherwise the holiness of God required destruction of the wicked state of Judah.

By example Jeremiah offers rich teaching on the nature and content of prayer. Through his personal suffering he ministers to those who experience persecution for the cause of Christ.

Anticipation

Jeremiah does not contain a rich menu of messianic prophecy like Isaiah. There are four passages in this book that speak directly of the coming of Christ. The most important of these prophecies is that Messiah will be the Righteous Shoot from the house of David (Jeremiah 23:5-6).

The most optimistic section of the book is found in chapters 30–33. In these chapters Jeremiah announces the survival of the house of David and the legitimate priesthood under a new covenant. The new covenant promise (31:31) is cited in the New Testament (Hebrews 8:8-13) as pointing to the Christian Age.

Keys

The key chapter in Jeremiah is chapter 25. In this chapter Jeremiah outlines the future of his people in the light of the rise of the powerful King Nebuchadnezzar. Judah and surrounding nations will serve the king of Babylon for seventy years. Then the king of Babylon will be required to drink the cup of God's wrath.

The key verse in the book is this: *"The time is coming," declares the LORD, "when I will make a new covenant with the house of Israel and with the house of Judah"* (Jeremiah 31:31).

The key phrases are *behold the days come* (14) and *a woman in travail* (8).

Key words in the book include *cry/weep* (35), *covenant* (24) and *daughter* (18).

Special Features

Jeremiah stands out from the other books in the Bible because of the following facts:

❖ Because of its size the Book of Jeremiah was positioned first in the books of prophets in some ancient manuscripts.

❖ Daniel studied the Book of Jeremiah in Babylon (Daniel 9:2). Daniel was particularly fascinated by Jeremiah's prophecy that Babylon would rule the world for seventy years (Jeremiah 25:11-14; 29:10).

❖ While the Book of Isaiah is generally in chronological order, the Book of Jeremiah often is not.

❖ There is more repetition in Jeremiah than in any other biblical book.

❖ Jeremiah's five "confessions" are poetic complaints to God and about God. They are unique in prophetic literature. These "confessions" are found in 11:18–12:6; 15:15-18; 17:12-18; 18:19-23; 20:7-13.

❖ While Isaiah was married, Jeremiah was commanded by the Lord not to marry (16:2).

❖ Jeremiah is the only Old Testament book that actually describes the way it came into being (ch. 36).

❖ Two seal impressions containing the names of characters mentioned in Jeremiah have been found in excavations in Jerusalem. One belonged to "Baruch son of Neriah the scribe" (32:12), the other to "Jerahmeel, King Jehoiakim's son," who was ordered to arrest Jeremiah and Baruch (36:36).

❖ The book contains correspondence with the exiles in Babylon (ch. 29).

❖ The first command to pray for the well-being of a foreign government is found in Jeremiah 29:7.

HEAR

Some have complained about how difficult it is to read Jeremiah because many of the passages are not in chronological order. In some ways, however, Jeremiah is an easy read. The exciting accounts of the prophet's vicissitudes during his five decades of ministry are compelling. The sermons of the prophet, filled as they are with brilliant metaphor, are pregnant with devotional application.

Here is a sampling of the outstanding chapters in Jeremiah:

- ❖ Catalog of Judah's sins (Jeremiah 2)
- ❖ Sin is a heart condition (Jeremiah 17)
- ❖ Avoid false prophets (Jeremiah 23)
- ❖ Confrontation between prophets (Jeremiah 28)
- ❖ Promises of a new covenant (Jeremiah 31)
- ❖ Some people never learn (Jeremiah 42–43)

Perhaps these famous lines from Jeremiah will stimulate you to search out other nuggets of truth in this book:

- ❖ *Can the Ethiopian change his skin or the leopard its spots? Neither can you do good who are accustomed to doing evil* (13:23).
- ❖ *I will put my law in their minds and write it on their hearts. I will be their God, and they will be my people* (31:33).
- ❖ *Like clay in the hand of the potter, so are you in my hand, O house of Israel* (18:6).
- ❖ *The heart is deceitful above all things and beyond cure* (17:9).
- ❖ *Let not the wise man boast of his wisdom or the strong man boast of his strength or the rich man boast of his riches, but let him who boasts boast about this: that he understands and knows me, that I am the* LORD (9:23-24).

25th Bible Book

Book of Lamentations
Facing Inexplicable Calamity

Originally the twenty-fifth book of the Bible took its title from the first Hebrew word in the book (also found in 2:1; 4:1). That word is *Ekhah*, which means *Alas*. Subsequently Jewish teachers gave the book the title *Qinoth*, which means *Laments*. In the Greek Bible the book was called *Lamentations*.

According to Jewish tradition the author of Lamentations was Jeremiah. This tradition is reflected in the full title of the Latin Bible: *The Lamentations of Jeremiah*. The tone and viewpoint of Lamentations is the same as the Book of Jeremiah. Also several verbal parallels between the two books have been identified.

The Book of Lamentations has received scant attention in Christian teaching. Children memorize the title as part of the books of the Bible. Few sermons or lessons, however, are based on this book. In general the body of Christ is not familiar with its contents. The book is like a stepchild within the family of biblical books. This is so because this book is perceived to be extremely somber and gloomy. The Lamentations are the painful outburst of a suffering people.

The Book of Lamentations contains five chapters, 154 verses, and 1,543 words.

Situation

Lamentations was written shortly after the fall of Jerusalem to Nebuchadnezzar in 586 BC. After a siege of eighteen horrible months, Nebuchadnezzar broke through Jerusalem's walls. King Zedekiah tried to escape. He was hunted down, captured, and taken to Riblah in Syria. There he watched his sons executed. Then his own eyes were put out, and he was taken to Babylon in chains. Jews were stunned when their Temple and capital were destroyed. They felt abandoned by God.

Lamentations describes the funeral of a city. The venerable city of David had now been reduced to rubble by the invading

Babylonian hordes. In a five-poem dirge, Jeremiah exposes the emotions of those who witnessed the disaster.

Plan

Structural plan. The Book of Lamentation consists of five independent poems. Chapters 1, 2, 3, and 4 are acrostic poems. There are twenty-two verses in chapters 1, 2, and 4, one for each letter of the Hebrew alphabet. Chapter 3 has sixty-six verses. Three verses in a row begin with succeeding letters of the Hebrew alphabet. With its twenty-two verses even the final chapter simulates an acrostic. The structure of Lamentations is displayed in the following chart.

Structure of Lamentations				
A Widowed City	A Broken People	A Suffering Prophet	A Ruined Kingdom	A Penitent Nation
Ch. 1	Ch. 2	Ch. 3	Ch. 4	Ch. 5
Acrostic Three-line Stanzas		Triple Acrostic	Acrostic Two-line Stanzas	Acrostic Simulated
Agony Growing		Agony Climax	Agony Subsiding	
Dirges				A Prayer

Geographical plan. Lamentations focuses on Jerusalem or Zion. The only other proper name in the book is Edom (4:21-22).

Eternal Purpose

The immediate purpose of Lamentations is to provide the congregation of Israel with a means by which they could express sorrow over their national loss. The deeper purpose of the book is to help God's people maintain their faith in the face of unspeakable tragedy.

The author wants his people to recognize the righteousness of God's dealings. He teaches them how to submit to the judgment that has befallen them. The author aims to lead back to God those who would not repent prior to the destruction of the city. He yearned for them to cast themselves upon the mercy of the Lord.

The Book of Lamentations intimates that Judah's loss can be traced to God's sovereignty and his justice. Lamentations is primarily a book about the terrible consequences of sin. Here we see the depths of human sorrow, not of one individual but of an entire community. Even the prayers recorded in Lamentations are desperate cries of anguish rather than affirmations of hope. The painful consequences of sin are lasting and deep.

Lamentations, however, is much more than the cheerless protest of the inequities of life. These poems are really an affirmation of faith in the justice and goodness of God. The author has experienced the worst that life can offer in the way of pain, sorrow, senseless violence, and loneliness. Yet his eye of faith penetrates the despair and focuses on the Living God. The Book of Job is designed to help believers cope with suffering on a personal level; Lamentations helps believers face calamities of massive proportions.

Anticipation

There is no personal messianic prophecy in Lamentations. The laments, however, remind us that over six centuries later Jesus was to weep over the impending destruction of that same city of Jerusalem by the Romans (Luke 13:34-35).

Keys

The key chapter in the Book of Lamentations is chapter 3. In the midst of the most intense lamentation of the book, the author's faith soars (3:22-25).

The key verse of the book is this: *his compassions never fail.* [23]*They are new every morning; great is your faithfulness* (Lamentations 3:22b-23).

The key phrase is *daughter of Zion* (8).

The key word is *sin/sins* (8).

Special Features

Some of the features that distinguish the Book of Lamentations within the biblical library are these:

❖ Originally Lamentations was appended to the Book of Jeremiah.

❖ In the modern Hebrew Bible Lamentations appears in the section called *Megilloth (Scrolls)* along with Esther, Ruth, Ecclesiastes, and Song of Solomon. Placement of the book in the English Bible follows the example of the Greek and Latin Bibles.

❖ Of the five chapters in this book, four have twenty-two verses. The only exception is chapter 3, which has sixty-six verses — three times twenty-two.

❖ Lamentations is the saddest book in the Bible, the only book made up entirely of mournful songs.

❖ This collection of laments, along with some heart-wrenching passages in the Book of Jeremiah, has earned Jeremiah the nickname, *the weeping prophet.*

❖ Many Jews today read Lamentations at the Western (Wailing) Wall, where they still lament the destruction of the Temple.

❖ The destruction of Jerusalem is at the heart of Jeremiah's two books. In the Book of Jeremiah the prophet looks ahead and warns of the destruction; in the Lamentations he looks back and reflects on the disaster.

HEAR

Through the cries of agony and descriptions of abandonment in Lamentations God speaks to us. We need to hear these words. They warn us about the consequences of sin. They set an example for us in how to cope with catastrophe. Here are a few of the outstanding verses in this book:

❖ *My sins have been bound into a yoke; by his hands they were woven together. They have come upon my neck and the Lord has sapped my strength. He has handed me over to those I cannot withstand* (1:14).

❖ *"The LORD is my portion; therefore I will wait for him." 25The LORD is good to those whose hope is in him, to the one who seeks him; 26it is good to wait quietly for the salvation of the LORD* (3:24-26).

❖ *It is good for a man to bear the yoke while he is young* (3:27).

❖ *Restore us to yourself, O LORD, that we may return; renew our days as of old* [22]*unless you have utterly rejected us and are angry with us beyond measure* (5:21-22).

Chapter Ten

FOCUS BOOKS (2)

Ezekiel–Daniel

W e have examined three of the so-called Major Prophets. In this chapter we will survey the last two of these books. The ministries of Ezekiel and Daniel overlap chronologically and geographically. Both of these books were written by Jewish prophets who had been transported to Babylon, Daniel in 604 BC, Ezekiel in 597 BC. Here the similarity ends. Daniel performed his ministry by interpreting dreams to Babylonian kings. Ezekiel was more like a pastor among the exiles in Babylon.

26th Bible Book
Book of Ezekiel
The Action Prophet

Ezekiel was the prophetic author of the twenty-sixth book of our Bible. The name means *God strengthens* or *God is strong*. He is the only person by this name in the Bible. The author's name only appears twice in this book (1:3; 24:24).

Ezekiel's father was a priest named Buzi. This means that in the normal course of events Ezekiel would have started his priestly ministry in the Temple at age thirty. That did not happen, however. God had bigger plans for this man.

Ezekiel was a married man. In fact the death of his wife occurred about the midpoint of his ministry.

The Book of Ezekiel contains forty-eight chapters, 1,273 verses, and 39,407 words. It is the third largest book in the Old Testament.

Situation

After his father Josiah was killed in battle, King Jehoiakim was installed on the throne in Jerusalem by Pharaoh Neco. When this Pharaoh was defeated by Nebuchadnezzar at the Battle of Carchemish in 605 BC, Jehoiakim hastily switched allegiance to the Babylonians. He rebelled against Nebuchadnezzar, however, after serving him for three years (2 Kings 24:1). By the time the Babylonian army arrived to punish him, Jehoiakim had died. His son Jehoiachin tried to rule, but lasted only about three months. In March of 597 BC the eighteen-year-old monarch surrendered Jerusalem to Nebuchadnezzar. Jehoiachin and ten thousand captives were taken to Babylon. Among them was Ezekiel.

After he had lived in Babylon for five years, God called Ezekiel to prophetic ministry among the captives. He was thirty at the time. In his call vision Ezekiel saw the throne-chariot of God (ch. 1). The year of his call was 593 BC.

For at least twenty-two years (and probably much longer) Ezekiel served among the thousands of Jewish captives in Babylon. Ezekiel has been dubbed *the action prophet* because of numerous bizarre antics that he used to get the attention of the captives and to drive his message home. The abundant use of these action parables sets him apart from all other prophets.

Ezekiel's message was similar to that of his contemporary Jeremiah who was preaching back in Jerusalem. At the same time Daniel was on the scene in Babylon. He is mentioned three times by Ezekiel (14:14, 20; 28:3). Daniel's ministry, however, was confined to the royal court.

The following events transpired in Babylon shortly before Ezekiel began to preach, or in the early years of his ministry there. First, Daniel began his ministry of dream interpretation (Daniel

2). Second, two Jewish false prophets were roasted in the fire by Nebuchadnezzar (Jeremiah 29:22). Third, Shadrach, Meshach, and Abednego were rescued from a similar fate (Daniel 3).

Plan

The Book of Ezekiel, like most prophetic books, is full of sermons and oracles interspersed with some narratives. What distinguishes this book, however, are the allegories/parables and visions found in the book.[3]

The material in the book is arranged in three divisions. The first twenty-four chapters contain Ezekiel's message concerning Jerusalem prior to the destruction of that city by Nebuchadnezzar in 586 BC. These chapters are full of condemnation and threats of catastrophe. The middle section of the book (chs. 25–32) contains Ezekiel's messages concerning Gentile nations. These mostly were penned during the eighteen months that Nebuchadnezzar besieged Jerusalem. The last division of the book (chs. 33–48) contains the prophet's message after the destruction of Jerusalem. These chapters are full of consolation and comfort. God had not abandoned his people.

From this analysis of the structure of the book it is clear that the most important event that transpired during Ezekiel's ministry was the fall of Jerusalem. Although Ezekiel did not personally go through this catastrophe as did Jeremiah, the news of it had a profound effect on the captives in Babylon. It nearly destroyed their faith.

Eternal Purpose

The immediate purpose of the Book of Ezekiel is twofold: to dash the delusion that Jerusalem could not be conquered and to comfort the captives after that disaster had occurred. The deeper purpose of the book is to depict in symbolic terms the glorious future of the people of God.

A casual perusal of this material has convinced many readers that Ezekiel has little spiritual value and even less contemporary

---

[3] The allegories/parables: 15:1-8; ch. 16; 17:1-21, 22-24; ch. 23; 24:1-14. The visions: 1:4-28; 2:9–3:13; 3:22-23; chs. 8–11; 37:1-10; chs. 40–48.

relevance. Those who attempt to make a more serious study of the book often fail to make it past the intricate visionary details of the first chapter. This is most unfortunate. Ezekiel has a vital message for God's people, a message not duplicated anywhere else in God's word.

Ezekiel surveyed the sins that required God's judgment upon Judah. He exposed the foolishness of false hopes of an early return to the homeland. God's judgment on Jerusalem and its Temple was certain to happen. Like Jeremiah, Ezekiel pounded away on this point.

When Jerusalem finally fell, Ezekiel comforted the exiles. He assured them of national restoration and future blessing under an eternal covenant. This emphasis on divine consolation is more detailed than that of Jeremiah.

The Book of Ezekiel is full of profound theology, not the least of which is the doctrine of individual responsibility (ch. 18). God's sovereign grace, his absolute holiness and justice, and his universality are presented here as clearly as in any other portion of Scripture. In spite of difficult details, the theme of ultimate victory for God's people is forcefully developed in this prophecy.

These mother-lode truths, plus priceless nuggets of revelation too numerous to mention will make the serious student of this book spiritually wealthy. Those who would prospect for this treasure should not be discouraged by the exegetical bogs which here and there challenge the resolve as well as the intellect.

Ezekiel offers a fascinating portrayal of God's heavenly glory (1:28; 3:12, 23). He saw that glory depart from the Jerusalem Temple (9:3; 10:4, 18-19; 11:22-23). Later he saw that divine glory return to a glorious temple that he envisioned for the future (43:1-5; 44:4).

Among the bizarre antics and perplexing visions of this book are clear and important insights about God. One of the most important of those insights is that God would rather forgive than punish. Because of his overall positive inclination toward people, God never gives up trying to win back the loyalty and love of those who have turned their backs on him.

Ezekiel saw himself as God's watchman. He felt responsible to warn his community of impending doom. His book reminds

Christians that we too are watchmen, called to urge others to turn to the Lord while there is still time.

Anticipation

There are at least four passages in Ezekiel that point directly to the Messiah. The prophecy marked * is the most important in the book.

❖ **The tender twig** (17:22-24)

❖ **The rightful king** (21:25-27)

❖ **The faithful shepherd** (34:23-31)*

❖ **The great reunion** (37:21-28)

Ezekiel envisioned a time when all of God's people were to be united under one king. He envisioned a wonderful temple from which the water of life was to flow forth to enliven the spiritually dead (symbolized by the Dead Sea). The temple portrayed by Ezekiel is Christ's temple—the church of Jesus Christ.

Keys

The key chapter in the Book of Ezekiel is chapter 37. In this chapter Ezekiel learned through a vision that God was about to resurrect the dry bones of his people Israel.

The key verse is this: *The soul who sins is the one who will die. The son will not share the guilt of the father, nor will the father share the guilt of the son* (Ezekiel 18:20a).

Without question the key phrase in the book is *son of man* (93), a phrase that designates Ezekiel as mortal man. Other prominent phrases are these: *they/you shall know* (61), *the word of the LORD came unto me* (49), and *glory of the LORD* (12).

Key words in the book include *sword* (82) and *measured* (33).

Special Features

There are many standout features of the Book of Ezekiel:

❖ Jesus' self-designation *son of man* may have been borrowed partly from the Book of Ezekiel.

❖ The name *Ezekiel* occurs only twice in this book and nowhere else in the Bible.

❖ God told Ezekiel *I have made you a sign to the house of Israel* (12:6). Ten sign sermons or action parables are recorded in the first twenty-four chapters[4] and one thereafter (37:15-17).

❖ The last word in the book is the symbolic name of the new Jerusalem: *Yahweh-shammah = Yahweh is there.*

❖ More visions and parables/allegories are used in this book than in any other Old Testament book.

❖ Ezekiel made two visionary flights to Jerusalem from Babylon. In the first he witnessed firsthand the appalling sins being committed secretly and in public by the nation's leaders (chs. 8–10). In the second (chs. 40–48) he saw a glorious future temple.

HEAR

While Ezekiel has been neglected by the church at large, it has come to be the happy hunting ground of cultists, critics, and curiosity mongers.

The modern biblical critics regard Ezekiel as pivotal in their topsy-turvy reconstruction of Old Testament history which views the Old Testament priesthood as a scribal concoction from Babylon rather than a divine revelation from Mount Sinai.

Ezekiel is cited by self-styled "students of prophecy" as proof that God's plan for the future includes the modern Zionist movement (Jews returning to Palestine in unbelief), an imminent Russian invasion of Israel, and the reinstitution of the Old Testament animal sacrificial system in a Temple shortly to be constructed in Jerusalem.

Science fiction buffs have scoured this book in search of spaceships and extraterrestrial beings who palmed themselves off as God.

Mormons regard Ezekiel 37:15-23 as the prophetic allusion to the Book of Mormon (stick of Ephraim) being joined to the Bible (stick of Judah).

---

[4] 4:1-3; 4:4-8; 4:9-17; 5:1-17; 12:1-7; 12:17-20; 21:1-17; 21:18-23; 22:17-31; 24:15-27.

If for no other reason the Book of Ezekiel merits careful study so that the servant of God may be able to silence these modern day *empty talkers and deceivers* who are upsetting so many families (Titus 1:10f.). The best defense against a thousand and one errors is the truth.

When you read Ezekiel for the first time you may wonder if this prophet was an eccentric — or worse, crazy. His behavior at times was nothing short of bizarre. Each of Ezekiel's dramatizations, however, added power to his message. You might forget some of his words, but you are not likely to forget Ezekiel's action parables. The book is a gallery of word pictures interspersed with ministages upon which the prophet performed divinely inspired monodramas. Ezekiel's delightful antics should draw students to his book in these days even as they attracted observers to his door in his day.

There is another warning of sorts to be made. Ezekiel was methodical in his writing style. He is meticulous about dating events, diligent in organization, and often repetitious. This somewhat wearisome framework, however, is permeated with a depth of mystery and richness of imagery and symbolism that will stimulate your imagination.

These outstanding chapters in Ezekiel will introduce you to the book:

❖ Ezekiel's encounter with a UFO (Ezekiel 1)
❖ Depiction of Judah's secret sins (Ezekiel 8–10)
❖ Doctrine of personal responsibility (Ezekiel 18)
❖ Ezekiel's appointment as watchman (Ezekiel 33)
❖ The dry bones passage (Ezekiel 37)
❖ Final battle against God's people (Ezekiel 38–39)
❖ The water of life (Ezekiel 47)

Some of the famous lines in this book are these:

❖ *Like mother, like daughter* (16:44).
❖ *Dem bones gonna rise again* (based on ch. 37).
❖ *There shall be showers of blessing* (34:26 KJV).
❖ *The fathers eat sour grapes, and the children's teeth are set on edge* (18:2).

27th Bible Book

Book of Daniel
The Statesman Prophet

The name *Daniel* means *God is my judge*. Two other Daniels are mentioned in the Bible. The author of this book came from the royal family of King David. In his youth Daniel was taken to Babylon as a hostage.

Daniel is one of the few well-known Bible characters about whom nothing negative is ever written. His life was characterized by faith, prayer, courage, consistency, and lack of compromise. Daniel is called by God's angel a man *greatly beloved* (9:23; 10:11, 19). Three times he is mentioned by his contemporary Ezekiel as a man of wisdom and righteousness (Ezekiel 14:14, 20; 28:3).

Throughout church history the Book of Daniel has been abused by its friends. Almost all of the many computations which men have made about the date of the Second Coming have been based on numbers found in Daniel. In certain cults like the Adventists and the Jehovah's Witnesses the prophecies of Daniel form the bedrock of their entire movement.

In Fundamentalist circles Daniel mania is prevalent. Those riding the prophetic hobby horse crank out literature on Daniel at a phenomenal rate. Televangelists hold audiences spellbound with messages on "Daniel's Seventieth Week" or "The Key to the Book of Daniel." Most of these interpreters come to the book with a prophetic "axe to grind." That is to say, they attempt to superimpose upon the book modern schemes of prophetic interpretation. Fanciful exegesis is supported by irrelevant cross-references based upon mere coincidence of terminology. Often Daniel is pried loose from its historical setting. Prophecies long since fulfilled to the letter are projected into the future. The result is that the vast majority of the voluminous literature on Daniel is largely worthless.

The book of Daniel contains twelve chapters, 357 verses, and 11,606 words.

Situation

Nebuchadnezzar became master of the world when he defeated the Egyptians at the Battle of Carchemish in 605 BC. He then swept southward through the region of Judah. He put Jehoiakim on the throne as his servant. As insurance against rebellion, Nebuchadnezzar took hostages, Daniel among them, to Babylon. Four of these hostages, including Daniel, were trained for the better part of three years for positions in the royal administration.

Daniel's ministry was restricted to the royal court at Babylon. He deciphered dreams for kings and recorded his own visions about the future. Daniel's prophetic career began in the second year of Nebuchadnezzar's reign (Daniel 2). This Hebrew served in the royal administrations of Nebuchadnezzar, Belshazzar, and the Persian Darius the Mede. His ministry concluded in the third year of Cyrus the Persian, about 536–535 BC.

These important events occurred during the lifetime of Daniel:

- ❖ **Battle of Carchemish** (605 BC)
- ❖ **Deportation of 10,000 Jews** (597 BC)
- ❖ **Destruction of Jerusalem** (586 BC)
- ❖ **Fall of Babylon to the Persians** (539 BC)

Plan

The Book of Daniel consists of several narratives. Nine of the twelve chapters revolve around dreams, including God-given visions involving trees, animals, beasts, and images. The book also contains royal proclamations and prophetic prayers.

Structural plan. The Book of Daniel has two natural divisions. Chapters 1–6 contain *narratives* illustrating the sovereign rule of God. Chapters 7–12 contain *prophecies* illustrating the same truth. In the first division Daniel interprets dreams; in the second, an angel interprets visions. Daniel's friends appear in the first division, but are not mentioned in the second. The first division is written in the third person, the second, in the first person.

Linguistic plan. The book is bilingual. Chapter 1 is written in Hebrew, chapters 2–7 are in the Aramaic language. Chapters 8–12 return to Hebrew. The key to this switch in languages is this: When Daniel speaks of God's people, he uses Hebrew. When he speaks concerning Gentile nations, he uses the international language of Aramaic.

Besides Daniel, the leading characters in the book are Daniel's three Hebrew friends **Shadrach, Meshach,** and **Abednego.** Three kings are important in the book: the Babylonian kings **Nebuchadnezzar** and **Belshazzar,** and the Persian king **Darius the Mede.** Two angels are involved in interpreting some of the visions: **Gabriel** and **Michael.**

Geographical plan. The setting of the entire book of Daniel is the region around Babylon. In his prophecies, however, Daniel speaks of great world kingdoms: Babylon, Medo-Persia, Greece, and Rome. Daniel also goes into detail predicting the political events that were to affect Judea during the intertestamental period. He speaks especially about how Judea was to be affected by the king of the south (Greek Ptolemaic kingdom of Egypt) and the king of the north (Greek Seleucid kingdom of Syria).

Eternal Purpose

The immediate purpose of the Book of Daniel is to demonstrate how God frustrates the plans of the mightiest monarchs and defends his servants in time of danger. The deeper purpose of the book is to show that it is God's ultimate purpose to end the trials of saints.

This book draws a contrast between the omnipotence of God and the impotence of the deities of Babylon. Furthermore, the book teaches that the course of history is determined by a divine plan. In God's own time the trials of the saints end. One day oppressors will be destroyed, and the saints will inherit the kingdom.

The central truth in this book is stated by Daniel himself: *the most High rules in the kingdom of men* (4:25; cf. 5:21). This is the great truth that Daniel taught Nebuchadnezzar in chapters 2 and 4, and of which he reminded Belshazzar in chapter 5. Nebuchadnezzar acknowledged this truth in chapter 4, and King Darius confessed it in chapter 6. The conviction of the sovereign rule of God undergirded Daniel's prayers in chapters 2 and 9, and his prophetic disclosures throughout the book. Confidence in the rule of God fortified Daniel's three friends when they defied the king's command and faced the fiery furnace (ch. 3).

Prophetically, Daniel is one of the most important of the biblical books. This book presents a surprisingly detailed and comprehensive sweep of prophetic history. Daniel discusses the rise and fall of Gentile world powers from his own day to the end of time.

Anticipation

Two great personal messianic prophecies are found in the Book of Daniel. First, one like a son of man is brought before the Ancient of Days and is given a kingdom (Daniel 7:14). In this passage *son of man* is used of one who ascends to heaven to rule eternally. This title emphasized humanity in the book of Ezekiel; but in Daniel it signifies deity. Hence, when Jesus referred to himself as *son of man* he was using a title that portrayed him as the God-man.

In the second great messianic prophecy the angel Gabriel announces that the Messiah will appear sixty-nine heptads (*weeks*) of years (= 483 years) after the command to restore Jerusalem (Daniel 9:25). This command was issued (presumably by Ezra) in 457 BC (Ezra 4:7-23). Jesus began his ministry at his baptism which occurred 483 years after the command to rebuild Jerusalem's walls.

Some think that Daniel 12:1-4 is referring to the ministry of Christ in figurative language. Daniel speaks of many who are dead (in sin) coming to life as in John 5:21, 25. He speaks of those who are wise (i.e., they accept Christ) shining like the brightness of the heavens.

Keys

The key chapter in the Book of Daniel is chapter 7. This chapter outlines the history of the world from Daniel's day to the end of time. It also sketches the history of God's kingdom from the enthronement of Christ to the ultimate triumph of his saints.

The key verse in the book is this: *the Most High is sovereign over the kingdoms of men and gives them to anyone he wishes* (Daniel 4:25b).

Key phrases in the book are *most High [God]* (13) and *God of heaven* (4).

The key word is *kingdom* (37).

Special Features

Here are some of the standout facts relating to the Book of Daniel:

❖ In the modern Hebrew Bible Daniel is found in the third division of books, the so-called *Kethubhim* or *Hagiographa*. English placement follows the Greek and Latin Bibles where Daniel is found following Ezekiel in the Major Prophets.

❖ Daniel is not called a *prophet* in his book. He was not regarded as a prophet by Jewish tradition. Jesus, however, called Daniel a *prophet* (Matthew 24:15).

❖ Two of the Bible's most famous stories are reported in this book: Daniel in the lions' den, and the three Hebrew men in the fiery furnace.

❖ Like the Book of Ezra, this book has chapters written in the international language of Aramaic rather than in Hebrew.

❖ Daniel is the only book in the Old Testament that gives the names of two angels: Gabriel and Michael.

❖ Daniel is the only book of the Bible to designate angels as *Watchers*.

❖ The Catholic Book of Daniel follows the Greek version and has three sizable additions. These are: *Bel and the Dragon; Susanna; Song of the Three Holy Children.* These additions were never part of the original Hebrew text. They do not properly belong in the book.

❖ According to the Jewish historian Josephus, Alexander the Great was diverted from destroying Jerusalem in 332 BC when he was shown the prophecies about him in the Book of Daniel.

❖ Daniel's life and ministry bridge the entire seventy-year period of Babylonian captivity.

HEAR

Some of the narratives in Daniel are familiar to many people who are not students of the Bible. Sunday School children are very familiar with the stories about Daniel and his companions in Babylon. Their fidelity to God in these seductive circumstances has encouraged believers through the ages. On the other hand, the prophetic portions of Daniel generally have been ignored in the educational program of the church. Unfortunately this material with its numerical symbolism and weird animal figures has been relegated to the happy hunting ground of full-time "students of prophecy."

Whatever one's position on the prophetic portions of Daniel, there are many rich lessons for living taught in this Old Testament book. Daniel rightly has earned his reputation as one of history's most admirable men. His experiences are without parallel in providing modern Christians with insight into principles of practical Christian living. Whether the focus of your interest is on magnificent prophecy or practical spiritual lessons, a study of the Book of Daniel will be a rewarding experience.

The Book of Daniel apparently was intended to comfort exiled Jews who were questioning whether the God of Bible was superior to the gods of Babylon and Persia. If allowed, however, this book could comfort all people. Through Daniel's stories and visions, God reminds us that he is truly the Most High and the All Powerful. He uses his power to stand by his people in lions' dens and fiery furnaces. He orchestrates history to the ultimate benefit of those who put their trust in him.

For a sample of what the Book of Daniel has to offer, spend a few minutes and read these chapters:

- ❖ Daniel interprets the king's dream (Daniel 2)
- ❖ Three fireproof boys (Daniel 3)
- ❖ God put Nebuchadnezzar out to pasture (Daniel 4)
- ❖ Handwriting on the wall (Daniel 5)
- ❖ Daniel in the lions' den (Daniel 6)

Here are a few of the outstanding verses in this book:

- ❖ *Daniel resolved not to defile himself with the royal food and wine* (1:8).
- ❖ *In the time of those kings, the God of heaven will set up a kingdom that will never be destroyed, nor will it be left to another people. It will crush all those kingdoms and bring them to an end, but it will itself endure forever* (2:44).
- ❖ *If we are thrown into the blazing furnace, the God we serve is able to save us from it, and he will rescue us from your hand, O king. [18]But even if he does not, we want you to know, O king, that we will not serve your gods or worship the image of gold you have set up* (3:17-18).
- ❖ *This is the inscription that was written: Mene, Mene, Tekel, Parsin [26]This is what these words mean: Mene: God has numbered the days of your reign and brought it to an end. [27]Tekel: You have been weighed on the scales and found wanting. [28]Peres: Your kingdom is divided and given to the Medes and Persians* (5:25-28).
- ❖ *Now when Daniel learned that the decree had been published, he went home to his upstairs room where the windows opened toward Jerusalem. Three times a day he got down on his knees and prayed, giving thanks to his God, just as he had done before* (6:10).

CHAPTER ELEVEN

FOCUS BOOKS (3)

Hosea–Amos

Having completed our survey of the Major Prophets, we now commence four lessons examining the smaller focus books — the so-called Minor Prophets. This group of twelve books is considered *minor* only in the sense that the individual books are smaller than those of Isaiah, Jeremiah, and Ezekiel. In Jewish tradition the entire group of twelve is considered as one book which is called simply *the Twelve.*

The books of the Minor Prophets have not been arranged in chronological order. They seem to have been placed in their present positions in order to highlight three main points of the prophetic message to Israel. The first division (Hosea thru Micah) focuses on the sin of Israel and the nations. The next division (Nahum thru Zephaniah) highlights the punishment of sin. The last division (Haggai thru Malachi) emphasizes the restoration that was to occur after the punishment of sin. The first three chapters of Hosea serve as a fitting introduction to the twelve Minor Prophets. These chapters address the same three points. Thus they serve to introduce the three major divisions of the collection.

28th Bible Book
Book of Hosea
Prophet of Love

The name Hosea means *salvation*. In the English Bible the name is spelled either *Hoshea* or *Hosea*. Four others by this name appear in the Bible.

Hosea's father is named Beeri. His wife was named Gomer. Hosea had three children to whom he gave symbolic names: *Jezreel* (*God scatters*), *Lo-ruhamah* (*no mercy*), and *Lo-ammi* (*not my people*). These names forecast God's future dealings with Israel.

Hosea has been called "the Jeremiah of the northern kingdom" (Kirkpatrick) and "the St. John of the Old Testament." His personal family tragedy has earned him the title "the man of shattered romance" (Ward). Because of his tender and earnest appeals for repentance he has been called "the home missionary," "the evangelist," and "the prophet of grace." His literary skills are recognized in the title "Israel's poet laureate."

The book contains fourteen chapters, 197 verses, and 5,175 words.

Situation

Hosea lived through the tumultuous decline of Israel (northern kingdom) after the prosperous reign of Jeroboam II. He began to prophesy about the time when Amos concluded his ministry, 752 BC. During this period the Assyrian Empire was bringing the Middle East to its knees.

Hosea's call to be a prophet came in the form of an unusual command from God: *Go, take to yourself an adulterous wife and children of unfaithfulness, because the land is guilty of the vilest adultery in departing from the LORD* (1:2). As a citizen of the northern kingdom of Israel Gomer was considered an adulterous wife, and the children she bore to Hosea were considered children of whoredom (unfaithfulness). The verse does not necessarily mean that Gomer personally was an immoral woman.

Hosea was a native of Ephraim or Israel (the northern kingdom). This prophet preached to the people of his own country. His ministry lasted about thirty-seven years, from about 752–715 BC. The aim of his ministry was to call God's wayward wife Israel to repentance by revealing the pain that Israel's unfaithfulness caused the Lord.

Hosea was a contemporary of the prophets Isaiah and Micah in Judah; Jonah and Amos in Israel.

Plan

The Book of Hosea begins with an action parable in which Hosea married and had children. His wife then deserted him. Hosea saw in this abandonment a picture of how Israel, God's figurative wife, had deserted her divine husband. The bulk of the book (chs. 4–14) consists of prophetic oracles and sayings of the prophet over the course of his lengthy ministry. Hosea expresses his message brilliantly. Few writers in the Old Testament can equal his skill and beauty.

Structural plan. The book breaks down into two major divisions: Hosea and his faithless wife (chs. 1–3); and Yahweh and his faithless people (chs. 4–14).

The second division is difficult to outline. The opening verse of the section may contain a clue to the organization. *Hear the word of the LORD, you Israelites, because the LORD has a charge to bring against you who live in the land: "There is no faithfulness, no love, no acknowledgment of God in the land"* (4:1). So chapters 4–14 contain three subdivisions, each of which concludes with an appeal for repentance. These subdivisions treat the lack in Israel of knowledge (4:2–6:3), mercy (6:4–11:11), and truth or covenant faithfulness (11:12–14:8).

Biographical plan. The leading characters in the book are Hosea and his family. Two others are mentioned in the messages of this prophet: King Shalman (short for Shalmaneser) and King Jareb (a symbolic name for the Assyrian king).

Geographical plan. Hosea focuses entirely on the fate of the northern kingdom of Israel.

Eternal Purpose

The immediate purpose of the Book of Hosea is to set before Ephraim/Israel the tragedy of national apostasy and the need for repentance. The deeper purpose of the book is to reveal the grace and compassion of God for his people.

Hosea utters about 150 statements concerning the sins of Israel, and more than half deal specifically with idolatry. These themes echo throughout the book: God's holiness vs. Israel's corruption, God's justice vs. Israel's injustice, God's love vs. Israel's hardness and empty ritual. The theme most appreciated by Christians is God's love for backsliders. The prophet had the marvelous ability to convey the anguish within the heart of a rejected God (cf. 2:14-15).

Hosea's family members are given symbolic significance in the book either because of their actions or because of the meaning of their names.

Family Member	Relationship	Symbolism
Gomer	Wife	Israel's unfaithfulness
Jezreel (*God Scatters*)	Son	Israel's defeat
Lo-Ruhamah (*Without Mercy*)	Daughter	Israel's abandonment
Lo-Ammi (*Not My People*)	Son	Israel's rejection

Anticipation

Christ is portrayed in Hosea in three ways: as the second Moses (Hosea 1:10-2:1), the second David (Hosea 3:5), and the second Israel (Hosea 11:1). In addition, Hosea anticipates the day when all of God's people will be united in one kingdom. He reversed the ominous names of his children to symbolize the day when God will sow (rather than scatter) his people, when those who had not before found mercy will find mercy, and those who were not God's people will become God's people (1:11-2:1; Romans 9:25f). He even foresaw the day when God will remove the sting of death (13:14; 1 Corinthians 15:55).

Keys

The key chapter in the Book of Hosea is chapter 1. The naming of Hosea's children in this chapter forms the springboard for all that is said in the rest of the book.

The key verse in the book is this: *How can I give you up, Ephraim?* (Hosea 11:8). This verse captures the aching heart of God as he contemplates judgment upon a nation that refused to repent. One could also argue that the key verse is 4:1 referenced above, because this verse outlines in reverse order the three great collections of Hosea's sayings (chs. 4–14).

The key phrase in Hosea is *my people* (10).

Key words include *Ephraim* (35), and *whoredom* or *prostitution* (9).

Special Features

Here are some interesting things about Hosea that set this book apart in the sacred collection:

❖ Hosea's name in Hebrew is almost identical to the names of Joshua and Jesus.

❖ Hosea was the only native of the northern kingdom (Ephraim/Israel) to record his prophetic messages to Israel.

❖ Like Isaiah, Hosea had two sons; but only Hosea names his daughter.

❖ Hosea is the only prophetic book that does not have some oracle against foreign nations.

HEAR

Hosea had real compassion for his people. His personal suffering because of Gomer's unfaithfulness gave him a unique insight into God's grief over Israel's sin. Thus, his words of coming judgment were tempered somewhat by the tenderness of his heart. Hosea used powerful metaphors to rebuke Israel for lying, murder, insincerity, ingratitude, idolatry, and covetousness. His messages, however, were always punctuated with consolation, passionate appeal, and future hope.

Here are some of the outstanding chapters in Hosea:

- ❖ Consequences of sin (Hosea 8–9)
- ❖ God's endless love (Hosea 11)
- ❖ The blessing of repentance (Hosea 14)

Some of the outstanding lines in the book are these:

- ❖ *They sow the wind and reap the whirlwind* (8:7).
- ❖ *You are not my people, and I am not your God* (1:9).

29th Bible Book
Book of Joel
Prophet of Pentecost

The name *Joel* means *Yahweh is God*. There are thirteen others by the same name in the Bible. All that is known about the author of Joel is that his father was Pethuel. Joel was probably a native of Jerusalem. Based upon the content of his book Joel has been called "the prophet of Pentecost" (Robinson), "the prophet of hopefulness," and "the prophet of the Spirit."

The Book of Joel contains three chapters, 73 verses, and 2,034 words.

Situation

In 841 BC Athaliah, daughter of Jezebel, seized the throne of Judah by killing all the royal family except an infant. She ruled for seven years. The surviving member of David's family was hidden in the Temple for those seven years. Then the high priest Jehoiada engineered a coup that overthrew Athaliah and restored the rightful ruler. He was a seven-year-old boy named Joash. During the minority of Joash, Jehoiada was regent. Many scholars think the period of Joash's minority is the time of Joel's ministry.

Joel's call is not recorded. It came, however, shortly after a terrible locust plague. Joel used that plague to announce a worse judgment to come.

Joel's ministry seems to have been rather short. It can be dated to about the year 830 BC.

Plan

The Book of Joel is made up entirely of prophetic oracles. Joel presents his message in majestic verse. He is regarded as one of the greatest poets in the Old Testament.

The book has two almost equal divisions dealing with God's judgment (1:1–2:17) and God's salvation (2:18–3:21). The former division consists of Joel speaking (38 verses). In these verses Joel describes the present devastation and announces a worse devastation to come (1:1–2:11). He then exhorts the people to repent (2:12-17).

In the second division God speaks (37 verses) of restoration of blessing (2:18-29), vindication through judgment (2:30–3:15), and glorification in the end (3:16-21).

Eternal Purpose

The immediate purpose of the Book of Joel is to explain a recent locust plague as a divine judgment on Judah. The deeper purpose of the book is to underscore the final blessings that will befall God's people, and the final disasters that will befall the enemies of God's people.

Joel used the locust plague as a springboard to announce the day of Yahweh, an even worse judgment to come. Joel stresses the sovereign power of Yahweh over nature and nations. He shares how God uses nature to get the attention of men. God was to bring against Judah something worse than locusts—an enemy as numerous as locusts. Joel warned the people of Judah of their need humbly to turn to the Lord with repentant hearts (2:12-17) so that God could bless rather than blast them. If they continued to spurn God's gracious call for repentance, judgment would be inevitable.

Because this book is among the earliest of the writing prophets, it contains the foundational statement of many of the most fundamental truths expressed in prophetic literature.

The doctrine of the day of Yahweh is the centerpiece of Joel's theology. Joel's outline of this event is expanded by later prophets, but these eight elements are part of the picture in this book: 1) signs and wonders in heaven; 2) the day of Yahweh is eschatological as well as historical—it depicts events at the end of time as well as events in present time; 3) great judgment is associated with that day; 4) it involves the final defeat and punishment of God's enemies, 5) the ultimate redemption of the remnant of believers, 6) the prominence of Zion, 7) Yahweh's triumphant and peaceful reign, and 8) the finality of this consummation.

Anticipation

One passage in Joel speaks directly of the coming of Messiah. In 2:23 Messiah is depicted as the *Teacher unto Righteousness* whose teaching will be like refreshing rain to the land.

Joel anticipates the day of Pentecost and the Christian Age that will commence with the outpouring of God's Spirit (2:28; Acts 2:16). He also speaks of a glorious new Jerusalem where Yahweh will dwell with his people forever (3:18-21).

Joel paints a beautiful picture of the new Jerusalem, one which is further developed in the New Testament. Six leading elements of his teaching in this regard are these: 1) the eternal safety of those who inhabit that city, 2) the holiness of Zion, 3) the absence of any stranger (unbeliever) there, 4) the presence of the river of the water of life, 5) the theme of eternal life, and 6) the fact that Zion is the habitation of Yahweh himself.

Keys

The key chapter in the Book of Joel is chapter 2. This chapter predicts the coming of the Teacher for Righteousness and the outpouring of God's Spirit in the last days.

The key verse in the book is this: *The day of the LORD is near; it will come like destruction from the Almighty* (Joel 1:15b).

The key phrases are *day of the LORD* (5) and *it shall come to pass* (3).

The key words include *day* (9) and *gather* (6).

Special Features

Here are some special attributes that make Joel stand out in the Bible:

❖ In the Hebrew Bible Joel is the second book of the Twelve; but in the Greek and Latin Bibles Joel stands fourth.

❖ While the English Book of Joel contains three chapters, in the Hebrew the verses are divided into four chapters.

❖ Joel prophesied during an unprecedented locust plague which served to forewarn the nation of an even greater catastrophe in the future.

❖ The only other mention of the prophet Joel in the Bible comes in a sermon by Peter on the day of Pentecost, when Peter declared that one of Joel's prophecies had just been fulfilled (Acts 2:16).

❖ This man of God was privileged to see in prophetic prospect both the beginning and the end of the Christian Age.

HEAR

Here is a sampling of the favorite verses in Joel:

❖ *Beat your plowshares into swords and your pruning hooks into spears* (3:10). The exact opposite of the scene in Isaiah (2:4) and Micah (4:3).

❖ *I will gather all nations and bring them down to the valley of Jehoshaphat. There I will enter into judgment against them concerning my inheritance, my people Israel* (3:2).

❖ *Multitudes, multitudes in the valley of decision* (3:14).

❖ *Rend your heart and not your garments* (2:13a).

❖ *Everyone who calls on the name of the* LORD *will be saved* (2:32).

❖ *I will pour out my Spirit on all people* (2:28).

❖ *In that day the mountains will drip new wine, and the hills will flow with milk. . . . A fountain will flow out of the* LORD's *house and will water the valley of acacias* (3:18).

30th Bible Book

Book of Amos
Prophet of the Plumb Line

The name *Amos* means *burden* or *burden bearer*. Only one other person by this name is mentioned in the Bible (Luke 3:25). The author of the thirtieth book of the Bible came from the small village of Tekoa, not far from Bethlehem in Judah. Amos earned his living by raising livestock and by harvesting sycamore figs (1:1; 7:14). He has been called "the cowboy prophet" (Phillips), "the Salvation Army prophet" (Kelso), and "the backwoods prophet" (Chappell). At best these designations are misleading, and at worst totally false. More appropriate are these designations: "the prophet of justice" (Robinson), "the prophet of righteousness," or "conscience incarnate."

The book which Amos left for posterity requires several important conclusions about this prophet. 1) He was well acquainted with the world of his day. He mentions the names of at least thirty-eight towns and districts of the ancient Near East. 2) He had a keen awareness of the history not only of his own people, but of foreign peoples as well. 3) He possessed a note of objectivity and sternness. 4) He was forthright in the presentation of the word of God. 5) He was a literary master and an incomparable preacher. His eloquent prose and poetry suggest he was more than a hired shepherd and farmhand. He was apparently an educated man, and perhaps the owner of a flock, some cattle, and a grove.

The Book of Amos contains nine chapters, 146 verses, and 4,217 words.

Situation

Amos began to preach during the very prosperous reign of Jeroboam II (793–753 BC). Business was booming. Kingdom boundaries were expanding. Below the surface, however, greed and injustice were festering. Hypocritical religious notions had replaced true worship. The nation had been lulled into a false sense of security. Attempts at divine discipline through famine, drought, plagues, death, and destruction had availed nothing.

Amos spoke powerfully of the social, moral, and religious corruption of the times. Religion in Israel had degenerated into empty ritualism. The golden calf, symbol of Yahweh worship in the north, had become nothing but an idol. Amos prophesied the destruction of the northern kingdom; but he did not specifically mention the agent of destruction. It is clear, however, that he had in mind the mighty Assyrian Empire.

The Book of Amos contains five visions that the prophet saw. Some scholars think that the first three of these visions (7:1-9) constituted Amos's call to prophetic ministry. His ministry appears to have been short. The dates 755–752 BC would not be far off.

Hosea was contemporary with Amos. What influence the short ministry of Amos may have had on Hosea is not known. Hosea seems to have received his call to preach about the time that Amos's ministry was winding down.

Plan

The Book of Amos contains visions, oracles, sermons, narrative, and even three hymn fragments.

Chronological plan. The Book of Amos is organized in two main blocks of material separated by a chapter that reveals the relationship between the two. The first six chapters focus on Amos's northern kingdom ministry (755–752 BC). In this material Amos delivers God's word of judgment against the nations (chs. 1–2) and his indictment of Israel (chs. 3–6). This first division concludes in 7:1-8 with the record of three visions Amos received explaining why he came from his home in Judah to preach in the north. The visions are followed by a short narrative that implies that Amos was expelled from the northern kingdom. The last two chapters contain two visions with accompanying messages which seem to have been preached in Judah. The Judean ministry probably lasted from 752–750 BC.

Biographical plan. The book alludes to three people: Amos the prophet, Amaziah the priest, and Jeroboam the king.

Eternal Purpose

The immediate purpose of the Book of Amos is to denounce the apostasy in Israel and to announce the coming judgment. The deeper purpose of the book is to foretell the future glory of David's kingdom.

Among the great truths taught by Amos are these. First, God holds even heathen nations accountable for their actions. Second, greater light requires greater accountability and more severe judgment. Third, true repentance is manifested in honest dealings with one's fellowman and justice in the courts. Fourth, Israel's hope for the future is wrapped up in the Davidic dynasty.

Amos was a stern critic of the social injustice that permeated the northern kingdom. The poor could not afford food and clothing. They were sold into debtors' slavery if they could not pay for a pair of sandals they had purchased on credit. Merchants took advantage of consumers with rigged scales. Judges sold favorable verdicts to the highest bidder. Amos championed the cause of the poor, the powerless, and the disadvantaged.

Anticipation

There is no personal messianic prophecy in Amos. In Amos 9:11, however, the prophet anticipates the restoration of the *tent* (dynasty) of David that had fallen. The family of David fell from power in 586 BC when the Babylonians destroyed Jerusalem. The Davidic dynasty was restored to power when the Lord Jesus, from the line of David, ascended to heaven and assumed his throne on the right hand of the Father (Hebrews 1:3). In highly poetic language Amos describes the kingdom of the future Ruler as one of unparalleled abundance and security (9:13-15).

Keys

The key chapter in the Book of Amos is chapter 7. This chapter is like a hinge that joins together the two major sections of prophetic messages.

The key verse in the book is this: *Prepare to meet your God, O Israel* (Amos 4:12b).

Key phrases in the book are these: *for three transgressions, yea for four* (8), *yet you have not returned unto me* (5), and *I will send a fire* (6).

Key words include *seek* (6), and *hear* (7).

Special Features

Like all the books of the Bible Amos has certain standout features:

- ❖ In the Hebrew Bible Amos stands third in the Twelve; in the Greek and Latin Bibles Amos has the second position.
- ❖ Amos prophesied two years before a great earthquake that took place in the days of King Uzziah (1:1). Over two hundred years later Zechariah referred to this same earthquake (Zechariah 14:5).
- ❖ Amos anticipates the destruction of Israel by the Assyrians, but he never mentions this adversary by name.
- ❖ Amos came from Judah, but most of his preaching was in the northern kingdom of Israel.
- ❖ Amos gained the attention of his hostile audience by issuing a series of brief oracles condemning neighboring nations for their crimes against humanity.

HEAR

Here are some favorite lines in the Book of Amos:

- ❖ *But let justice roll on like a river, righteousness like a never-failing stream* (5:24). The favorite text of Martin Luther King, Jr.
- ❖ *The lion has roared – who will not fear? The Sovereign LORD has spoken – who can but prophesy?* (3:8).
- ❖ *Woe to you who are complacent in Zion* (6:1).
- ❖ *I am setting a plumb line among my people Israel* (7:8)
- ❖ *I was neither a prophet nor a prophet's son* (7:14).
- ❖ *I will send a famine through the land – not a famine of food or a thirst for water, but a famine of hearing the words of the LORD* (8:11).
- ❖ *Are not you Israelites the same to me as the Cushites?* (9:7).

CHAPTER TWELVE

FOCUS BOOKS (4)
Obadiah–Micah

n the previous chapter we surveyed the first three of the Minor Prophets: Hosea, Joel, and Amos. In this chapter we shall get acquainted with the books of Obadiah, Jonah, and Micah. Keep in mind that the first six books of the Minor Prophets are not arranged in chronological order.

31st Bible Book
Book of Obadiah
Prophet of Edom's Doom

The name *Obadiah* means *servant of Yahweh*. Twelve others by the same name are mentioned in the Old Testament. Nothing is known about this Obadiah. He probably was a citizen of Judah.

Obadiah has been called "the antagonist of Edom," "the censurer of ridicule" and "the prophet of poetic justice." His critics accuse him of "provincialism," and "intense sectionalism."

The Book of Obadiah contains one chapter, twenty-one verses, and 670 words. This book — more of a tract than a book — is the shortest among the Minor Prophets. Yet the importance of the message of this unheralded herald is disproportionate to the length of his writing.

Situation

There are few clues about the circumstances that led Obadiah to write his book. Jerusalem had recently been sacked by enemies; yet the description of this event does not measure up to the devastation inflicted by the Babylonians in 586 BC. During the reign of King Jehoram of Judah (848–841 BC) Jerusalem was sacked by a coalition of Philistines and Arabians (2 Chronicles 21:16-17). The Edomites took advantage of Judah's weak condition at this time. It is this sack of Jerusalem that forms the backdrop of Obadiah's writing.

Of Obadiah's ministry only this short message concerning Edom survives.

Plan

The Book of Obadiah is one prophetic oracle. It is organized into three divisions: a pronouncement against Edom (vv. 1-10), a prediction regarding the nations (vv. 15-16), and a promise to Israel (vv. 17-21). In the first division God's people are violated, in the second they are validated, and in the third they are vindicated.

Although Obadiah was a Judean prophet, the focus of his message was Edom. This country was located almost due south of the Dead Sea. The region was very mountainous and isolated. During biblical history the Edomites and Israelites at times were allies, at times were adversaries. At the time this book was written these two nations were supposed allies or *brothers* as the text calls them.

Eternal Purpose

The immediate purpose of the Book of Obadiah is to show that Edom's actions against Judah will be punished, but God's people will be glorified. The deeper purpose of the book is to show that the kingdom of God ultimately will be triumphant.

The message of Obadiah might be titled "A Tale of Two Mounts." In this book Mount Zion represents the people of God. Mount Esau represents the adversaries of God's people. The same contrast is found in the terminology *house of Jacob* and *house of Esau.*

For Mount Zion the present is bleak, but the future is bright. On the other hand, Mount Esau (the adversaries of God's people) has no future at all. For Edom there are no pleas to return, no words of consolation or hope. Edom's doom is sealed. There are no conditions for possible deliverance. God will bring total destruction upon Edom. There will be no remnant. The Judge of the earth will overthrow the pride of Edom and restore the house of Jacob.

Anticipation

There is no personal messianic prophecy in Obadiah. There is, however, the grand hope that God's kingdom will be a place of deliverance (v. 17). The kingdom of Christ is the Mount Zion of the latter days (Hebrews 12:22).

Keys

The key verse in the Book of Obadiah is the final one: *And the kingdom will be the LORD's* (21b).

The key phrase is *the day of* (4).

Key words include *Esau* (7) and *mount* (6).

Special Features

Here are some special features of the little book of Obadiah:

- ❖ In the Hebrew Bible Obadiah is the fourth book of the Twelve. In the Greek and Latin Bibles Obadiah has the fifth position.
- ❖ Chronologically Obadiah is the first prophet to introduce the theme of *the day of Yahweh*. The theme was further developed by Joel and Amos.
- ❖ Jeremiah alluded to Obadiah 1-5 in condemning Edom in his day more than two hundred years after Obadiah.
- ❖ The Edomites, the subject of this book, were descendants of Esau, the twin brother of Jacob (Israel).
- ❖ Obadiah is the shortest book of the Old Testament; but it carries one of the strongest messages of judgment.
- ❖ Edom was famous for its wise men. One of Job's well-educated friends came from there (Job 2:11).
- ❖ Many think that Obadiah is the earliest of Israel's writing prophets.

HEAR

Here are some of the favorite lines from Obadiah:

❖ *The day of the LORD is near for all nations* (15a).
❖ *As you have done, it will be done to you: your deeds will return upon your own head* (15b).

32ⁿᵈ Bible Book
Book of Jonah
Prejudiced Prophet

The name *Jonah* means *dove*. The prophet Jonah is also mentioned in 2 Kings 14:25. Jonah was the son of Amittai (1:1). He came from the town of Gath-hepher about three miles north of Nazareth in Galilee.

The Book of Jonah contains four chapters, forty-eight verses, and 1,321 words.

Situation

Jonah was the most popular prophet of his day. He might well be called a patriot. Jonah was a resident of Israel. His was the happy task of predicting the military successes won by Jeroboam II, and the great prosperity of his era (2 Kings 14:25). His optimistic predictions encouraged King Jeroboam to recover lost Israelite territory.

In Jonah's day the rising power to the east was Assyria. The Assyrians were noted for the ruthless atrocities that they committed in warfare. About 755 BC God dispatched Jonah to convey to the city of Nineveh in Assyria a message of warning about impending doom. The prophet rebelled against this assignment. Jonah fled in the opposite direction!

Jonah's ministry invites comparison with that of Elijah. The accounts of both prophets are thoroughly supernaturalistic. Both had their lives preserved by miracles. Both converted large numbers. God found it necessary to discipline Elijah. The same is true of Jonah. Both prophets were impatient with God. Both desired to see the wicked suddenly and miraculously overthrown. Both accounts end with the prophet engaging in personal conversation with God. Neither account explicitly mentions a change of negative attitude on the part of the prophet.

Plan

The Book of Jonah is mostly narrative. There is one brief (five words in the Hebrew) oracle, and a psalm that functions as a prayer.

The Book of Jonah is divided in two major sections, which can be labeled *the saving of a sinner* (chs. 1–2) and *the saving of a city* (chs. 3–4).

Geographically, each chapter of the book has a different setting. In chapter 1 Jonah is on a ship sailing for Tarshish. In chapter 2 he is within a great fish in the Mediterranean Sea. In chapter 3 Jonah is preaching in Nineveh. In chapter 4 he is outside the city waiting to see what became of the Ninevites' repentance.

Eternal Purpose

The immediate purpose of the Book of Jonah is to teach that God's mercy and compassion extend even to the heathen. The deeper purpose of the book is to set forth a type (picture/preview) of Christ's burial and resurrection.

The Book of Jonah is perhaps the most controversial book in the Old Testament, if not the entire Bible. The book is full of miracles, and that offends the rationalistic mind of modern man. This book, however, emphasizes more than any other the universal love of God. It is interesting that pagan Nineveh responded more readily to the preaching of Jonah than Israel and Judah ever responded to any prophet of God.

Through the experiences reported in this book, Jonah learned a number of principles. First, Jonah learned that it is impossible to succeed in running away from God. Second, he came to realize that there is no limit to what God will do to get the attention of a rebellious saint. Third, Jonah found out that God is in the business of giving second chances. Fourth, he discovered that disobedience to God creates turmoil in the life of a believer.

The book is full of other important lessons for believers. Here are a few of them. 1) The book is a rebuke to those who long for the conversion of sinners provided that they can select the sinners to be converted. 2) The book also rebukes those who do not have the passion to win people to Christ. 3) The person who questions the wisdom of God posits for himself a wisdom that exceeds omniscience. 4) The way to Nineveh may seem hard, and the way to Tarshish full of promise; but God knows best. 5) Human beings and even dumb beasts are all precious in the sight of God. 6) Are believers more concerned about plants or people? 7) God's love is great in its downward reach and in its outreach. 8) No preacher is qualified to preach to all men if he is not ready to preach to any man.

The character of Jonah has been described as self-determined and self-centered. Two commendable characteristics of the man were his frankness and his honesty. Whatever negative assessment is made of Jonah's life, he was not guilty of hypocrisy. He was narrow in his outlook, in fact he was nationalistic, totally unconcerned about the spiritual condition of those outside Israel. With all of his faults, however, Jonah was still teachable.

Perhaps one of the most fascinating lessons of this book is seen in the timing of Jonah's experience, during the reign of Jeroboam II. It was during this same reign that Amos confronted the rich of Israel. He condemned the social injustice that developed with prosperity. Like Jonah, Amos also announced judgment. He called on the people of God to repent. The significance of Jonah's mission is that God's grace toward Nineveh served as a vivid object lesson for Israel. If God's people like Nineveh would repent Israel too could be saved. Ironically, although Jonah did not realize it, his mission to Nineveh was at the same time a mission to Israel as well.

Anticipation

There is no direct prophecy concerning the coming of Christ in the Book of Jonah. There is, however, the next best thing. Jonah's entombment in the belly of the fish for three days and nights is a type (preview/picture) of the entombment of Jesus in the heart of the earth. *He answered, "A wicked and adulterous generation asks for a miraculous sign! But none will be given it except the sign of the prophet Jonah. ⁴⁰For as Jonah was three days and three nights in the belly of a huge fish, so the Son of Man will be three days and three nights in the heart of the earth. ⁴¹The men of Nineveh will stand up at the judgment with this generation and condemn it; for they repented at the preaching of Jonah, and now one greater than Jonah is here* (Matthew 12:39-41).

Keys

The key chapter in the Book of Jonah is chapter 3. This chapter records the greatest revival of all time. The repentance of the Ninevites probably occurred during the reign of the Assyrian King Ashurdan III (773–755 BC).

The key verse in this book is this: *Forty more days, and Nineveh will be overturned* (3:4b).

The key phrase in the book is *God provided* (4).

The key word is *Nineveh* (9).

Special Features

Here are some interesting facts relating to the Book of Jonah:

- ❖ In the Hebrew Bible the Book of Jonah is in fifth position in the Book of the Twelve. In the Greek and Latin Bibles Jonah stands sixth.
- ❖ Jonah is unique among the prophetic books in that it consists largely of narrative.
- ❖ The Pharisees were wrong when they said: *Look into it, and you will find that a prophet does not come out of Galilee* (John 7:52). Jonah was from Galilee.
- ❖ One (unlikely) Jewish tradition says that Jonah was the son of the widow of Zarephath whom Elijah raised from the dead (1 Kings 17:8-24).
- ❖ Here and there Jonah makes use of Aramaic words in this book.
- ❖ Jonah is the only prophet to whom Jesus likened himself (Matthew 12:39-41).

❖ Unlike other prophetic books, Jonah places more emphasis on the messenger than the message.

❖ Jonah was the only prophet sent directly to the Gentiles, and the only prophet who rebelled against his mission.

❖ Of all the people and things mentioned in the book — the storm, the lots, the sailors, the fish, the Ninevites, the plant, the worm, and the east wind — only the prophet himself failed to obey God.

HEAR

Here are some of the favorite lines from the Book of Jonah:

❖ *But the LORD had provided a great fish to swallow Jonah, and Jonah was inside the fish three days and three nights (1:17).*

❖ *From inside the fish Jonah prayed to the LORD his God (2:1).*

❖ *God . . . had compassion and did not bring upon them the destruction he had threatened (3:10).*

❖ *But Nineveh has more than a hundred and twenty thousand people who cannot tell their right hand from their left, and many cattle as well. Should I not be concerned about that great city? (4:11).*

33rd Bible Book
Book of Micah
Prophet of the Downtrodden

The name *Micah* means *who is like Yahweh?* Five different spellings of this name are found in the Bible. Six different men wear this name. The author of the prophetic book is identified by his hometown. Morashah was a country village of Judah about twenty-five miles southwest of Jerusalem. Hence Micah is called *the Morasthite* (Micah 1:1).

Micah has been called "the homely country prophet," "worthy champion of the poor" (Yates) and "the spokesman for the common people" (Blackwood). Perhaps of all the prophets Micah is the one whose contributions have been least appreciated. Yet in Micah the Morasthite there is combined Amos's passion for justice and Hosea's heart of love. In this book are some of the most outstanding prophecies in the Old Testament.

The Book of Micah contains seven chapters, 105 verses, and 3,153 words.

Situation

Beginning in 745 BC the Assyrian Empire under Tiglath-pileser made itself master of the world. Judah voluntarily rendered tribute to Assyria as early as 734 BC when King Ahaz sought the aid of Tiglath-pileser. Good King Hezekiah cast off the Assyrian yoke and brought down upon Judah the wrath of the Assyrian King Sennacherib in 701 BC.

Micah lived in the region around Jerusalem. He began to prophesy about 735 BC. His ministry continued for about thirty-four years, down to 701 BC when his major predictions concerning the fate of Judah began to materialize. Chronologically, the ministry of Micah paralleled that of Isaiah.

Plan

The Book of Micah consists largely of prophetic oracles supplemented with laments and dialogue with the sinners. The book is divided into three sermons each distinguished from the other by the word *hear* (1:2; 3:1; 6:1). The first sermon is directed to the nations (chs. 1–2), the second to the rulers (chs. 3–5), and the third to Israel (chs. 6–7).

There is balance of content in this book. One-third of Micah's book exposes the sins of his countrymen; another third pictures the punishment God is about to send; and the final third holds out the hope of restoration once that discipline has ended.

Geographically Micah mostly focused on his native land of Judah. His sermons were delivered for the most part on trips to Jerusalem. He does include in his book one brief oracle concerning Samaria, capital of the northern kingdom of Israel.

Eternal Purpose

The immediate purpose of the Book of Micah is to correct inequity and injustice in the land through censure and threat of judgment. The deeper purpose of this book is to portray the ultimate government of God in the land through the coming Ruler to be born in Bethlehem.

The Book of Micah contains several contrasting theological emphases. To Micah Yahweh is the God of Israel, yet at the same time the God of all nations. Yahweh is Judge, yet he is also Savior. He is majestic in wrath, yet astonishing in compassion. He demands and executes justice, yet promises forgiveness. Yahweh scatters, but also gathers his flock. He destroys Zion, yet he also resurrects Zion. The God of Micah threatens the nations with humiliation, yet offers those same nations peace.

In a sense Isaiah and Micah were God's one-two punch in the last decades of the eighth century before Christ. Both prophets addressed the same people and problems. If Isaiah stressed faith, Micah stressed works. Both prophets saw Yahweh as Ruler of nations and men. Both recognized the absolute holiness and majesty of the Lord. The vision of the great Temple mount is presented verbatim by both prophets (Isaiah 2:2-4; Micah 4:1-3). In some ways, Micah is Isaiah in miniature; but there is this difference in emphasis. Micah focused on moral and social problems while Isaiah placed greater stress on world affairs and political concerns.

A synopsis of Micah looks like this: Three times Micah warns the Jews that their nation will die. Then he promised a great act of deliverance. One day the nation will be restored. Restoration will come not because the Jews deserved it, but because of the grace of God.

Anticipation

Two passages in Micah qualify as personal messianic predictions. First, in 2:12-13 Messiah breaks through barriers to lead his people out of bondage. Second, in 5:1-5, Micah predicts the birth of a great future Ruler in Bethlehem. Micah also describes the

Messiah's kingdom in the last days — a kingdom that will attract the Gentiles (4:1-4).

Keys

The key chapters in the Book of Micah are chapters 6-7. In these chapters Israel is condemned in a courtroom scene; yet God in mercy extends hope to his people.

The key verse in the book is this: *He has showed you, O man, what is good; and what does the* LORD *require of you? To act justly and to love mercy and to walk humbly with your God?* (6:8).

Key phrases in the book are *my people* (9), and *in that day* (5). The key word in Micah is *hear* (9).

Special Features

Here are some facts about the Book of Micah that distinguish it in the sacred collection:

❖ In the Hebrew Bible Micah is in the sixth position within the Book of the Twelve. In the Greek and Latin Bibles Micah is in the third position.

❖ The Book of Micah is quoted three times in later biblical history: 1) by the elders of Judah in order to save Jeremiah's life (Jeremiah 26:18; cf. Micah 3:12), 2) by the chief priests and scribes in Jesus' day (Matthew 2:5-8; cf. Micah 5:2), and 3) by Jesus when sending out the twelve (Matthew 10:35; cf. Micah 7:6).

❖ The opening chapter in the Hebrew contains a series of wordplays on the names of villages of Judah by which Micah prophesies the invasion of the Assyrians (Micah 1:10-16). This wordplay is difficult to bring out in English translation.

❖ Like Isaiah, Micah may have walked around "naked" for a time in order graphically to depict the fate of prisoners being taken into captivity. See 1:8; cf. Isaiah 20:1-4.

❖ Micah had a clear understanding of his inspiration by the Spirit of God (3:8).

HEAR

Here are some of the favorite lines from the Book of Micah:

- ❖ *They will beat their swords into plowshares and their spears into pruning hooks. Nation will not take up sword against nation, nor will they train for war anymore.* (4:3b).
- ❖ *Bethlehem Ephrathah . . . out of you will come for me one who will be ruler over Israel* (5:2).
- ❖ *But as for me, I am filled with power, with the Spirit of the* LORD, *and with justice and might, to declare to Jacob his transgression, to Israel his sin* (3:8).
- ❖ *You will again have compassion on us; you will tread our sins underfoot and hurl our iniquities into the depths of the sea.* (7:19).

CHAPTER THIRTEEN

FOCUS BOOKS (5)
Nahum–Zephaniah

n the two previous lessons we surveyed the first six of the books of the so-called Minor Prophets. These books come from the pre-Assyrian (Obadiah, Joel) and Assyrian (Hosea, Amos, Jonah, Micah) periods. The next three books on this Focus shelf have two things in common. First, each has only a trio of chapters. Second, all three books come from the seventh century before Christ, the silver age of Hebrew prophecy.

34th Bible Book
Book of Nahum
Prophet of Nineveh's Doom

The name *Nahum* means *comfort*. This prophet is the only one by this name in the Bible. His name, however, is a shortened form of *Nehemiah* (*comfort of Yahweh*). The name of this prophet is appropriate for the message. This messenger brought comfort to God's people when he announced that the century-long oppression by the Assyrians was about to be crushed.

Nothing more is known about the personal life of Nahum except that he was from the town of Elkosh. The location of this village is uncertain.

Because of the subject matter of his book, Nahum has been called "the prophet of Nineveh's doom" (Huffman) and "the critic of Nineveh" (Ward). His skill as a poet has earned him the designation "the tragic poet" (Scofield) and "poet laureate of the Minor Prophets" (Patterson and Travers).

The Book of Nahum contains three chapters, 47 verses, and 1,285 words.

Situation

The powerful message of Nahum is enhanced when placed alongside the message of Jonah. Through the preaching of Jonah God warned the Ninevites of impending judgment. He spared that great city when the citizens responded positively to the warning. The conversion of the Ninevites took place about 755 BC.

No matter how sincere the revival in Nineveh may have been, it was short-lived. The Assyrians soon returned to their ruthless ways. In 722 BC King Sargon II of Assyria destroyed Samaria, the capital of the northern kingdom of Israel. He deported and scattered the ten tribes of the north. Under King Sennacherib, the Assyrians almost captured Jerusalem in 701 BC.

The last great king of Assyria was Ashurbanipal (669–633 BC). About a decade before Nahum came on the scene, the Assyrians had extended their empire to its greatest extent. They had captured the major Egyptian capital of Thebes (664 BC). After Ashurbanipal's reign, however, the Assyrian Empire gradually crumbled.

By 632 BC Judah was able to regain its independence under good King Josiah. This king launched the last and most thoroughgoing reformation described in the Old Testament. The revival effort reached its climax in 621 BC with the discovery of a lost law book in the Temple. During this period God called upon Nahum to announce the impending doom of Nineveh, one of the capitals of Assyria.

Nahum frequently addresses Nineveh in the book. His intended audience, however, was the oppressed people of God. For over a century they had suffered at the hands of the brutal Assyrian armies. God's people had seen their homes destroyed, their crops burned, their neighbors deported in chains, their wealth confiscated, their women raped, and their children dashed against stone walls.

One must understand this background in order to have the right perspective on Nahum. This is not an orgy of hatred, as some have called it. Nahum is an announcement of just retribution. Through the use of the Assyrians God had meted out severe punishment upon the sins of his people. Now it was time for those oppressors to meet their Maker in judgment. So Nahum is a cry of praise celebrating the justice of God.

Nahum's ministry took place in Judah. We can estimate that Nahum had a ministry of about thirty years extending from about 654 to 624 BC.

The prophets who were on the scene about the same time as Nahum were Zephaniah, Jeremiah, and Habakkuk.

Plan

The Book of Nahum consists entirely of prophetic oracles. The three chapters reflect the outline of the book:

❖ **Verdict against Nineveh** (ch. 1)

❖ **Vision of Nineveh's fall** (ch. 2)

❖ **Vindication of Nineveh's fall** (ch. 3)

One could also say that in these three chapters Nineveh's judgment is declared, described, and defended.

From the above it becomes obvious that Nahum is a single-focus book. His subject is Nineveh, located in what is now Iraq. By the time of Nahum, Nineveh had become the mightiest city on earth. Its walls are said to have been a hundred feet high. They were wide enough to accommodate three chariots riding abreast. Here and there around the walls were huge towers that reached an additional hundred feet above the top of the walls. For added protection the walls were surrounded by a moat 150 feet wide and 60 feet deep. Nineveh seemed impregnable. Military experts thought the city could withstand a siege of twenty-years. Thus, Nahum's prediction of Nineveh's imminent overthrow seemed unlikely indeed.

Eternal Purpose

The immediate purpose of the Book of Nahum is to pronounce the doom that was about to fall on Nineveh. The deeper purpose of the book is to set forth God's righteous wrath against all oppressors.

Nahum is largely ignored by believers because there seems to be little here that applies directly to Christian experience. Yet this little book sets forth some basic theological values. This is a moral universe. Ultimately right is rewarded and wrong punished. God is moral judge, not only of his people but of the whole world. He is both able and willing to judge sin wherever it is found.

Nahum focuses on God's righteous judgment on one of the most ruthless people that ever lived on the earth. He expresses the relief and gratitude of all God's people over the prospect of the fall of the international bully that had humiliated them and mocked their God for decades. Nineveh was the Goliath of the time, a Goliath that was about to be whittled down to size by David's God.

Nahum was very specific in what he said would happen to the great city. Nineveh was to be destroyed by flood (1:8; 2:6) and fire (1:10; 2:13; 3:13, 15). Nahum described the profaning of Nineveh's temples and images (1:14). He announced that the city never would be rebuilt (1:14; 2:11, 13). Nahum depicted the leaders of Nineveh fleeing in the face of an enemy (2:9; 3:17). He spoke of the easy capture of the fortresses around the city (3:12), the destruction of the gates (3:13), the lengthy siege and the frantic efforts to strengthen the city's defenses (3:14).

Nineveh fell in 612 BC. It was so thoroughly obliterated that its very location was questioned for centuries. Modern archeologists, however, have unearthed this once-proud capital of the world. The light that archeology has shed on the final days of Nineveh has verified all that Nahum predicted about the place.

Anticipation

There is no personal messianic prophecy in Nahum. When one reads the attributes of God in 1:2-8, however, he inevitably thinks of the work of Christ as the Judge of nations at the end of time.

Keys

The key chapter in the Book of Nahum is chapter 1. This chapter records the principles of divine judgment that required the destruction of Nineveh.

The key verse in the book is: *The L*ORD *takes vengeance on his foes and he maintains his wrath against his enemies* (1:2b).

The key phrase in the book is *cut off* (3).

Key words include *like* (5) and *Nineveh* (3).

Special Features

Here are some of the peculiar facts that make Nahum stand out in the Bible.

❖ There are only forty-seven verses in this book, but it contains nearly fifty references to nature.

❖ Nahum is not quoted in the New Testament.

❖ This book does not contain one word of condemnation against Judah. It has no call to repentance or reformation.

❖ Nahum is one of the three prophets who primarily focused on the judgment of Judah's enemies. The other two are Obadiah (Edom) and Habakkuk (Babylon).

HEAR

Here are some favorite lines from the Book of Nahum:

❖ *The L*ORD *is slow to anger* (1:3).

❖ *The L*ORD *is good, a refuge in times of trouble* (1:7).

35ᵗʰ Bible Book

Book of Habakkuk

Prophet of the Watchtower

The name Habakkuk means *embraced*. He is the only person by this name in the Bible. Nothing is known about the personal life of the man. The statement at the end of the psalm in chapter 3 (*To the chief Musician. With my stringed instruments.*) suggests that he may have been a priest connected with the Temple worship in Jerusalem.

Habakkuk has been called "the optimist" (Ward), "the philosopher" (Robinson), "philosophic prophet" (Scofield), and "the prophet of persistent faith" (Tesh). The character of this prophet and the nature of his prophecy are sadly misrepresented in such designations as "the father of speculation," "the skeptic," "the father of modern religious doubt," or "the freethinker among the prophets."

The Book of Habakkuk contains three chapters, fifty-six verses, and 1,476 words.

Situation

In 612 BC Nineveh, capital of Assyria, fell to a combined army of Medes and Babylonians. Fearing a shift in the balance of international power, Pharaoh Neco came to the Euphrates River to bolster the tattered remnants of the Assyrian army. Finally in 605 BC Nebuchadnezzar of Babylon defeated the Egyptian army and became master of the world. In the context of the rise of Babylon, Habakkuk was called to be God's prophet.

Habakkuk lived in Judah. He began to prophesy about 609 BC just before the showdown between Egypt and Babylon at the Battle of Carchemish. Habakkuk's ministry continued for about nine years to about 600 BC.

Prophets contemporary with Habakkuk were Jeremiah, Zephaniah, and Nahum.

Plan

The Book of Habakkuk contains a dramatic dialogue between the prophet and God, oracles, and a prayer/song. The three chapters outline the contents. In chapter 1 Habakkuk complained to God about sinful conditions in Judah. The Lord indicated that Judah would be punished by means of the Chaldeans or Babylonians. In chapter 2 Habakkuk listened to God. He learned that eventually God would punish Babylon. In chapter 3 Habakkuk prayed. He describes the power of God. Another way of expressing this same outline is this:

❖ **Faith faces a problem** (ch. 1)

❖ **Faith finds a solution** (ch. 2)

❖ **Faith full of assurance** (ch. 3)

Eternal Purpose

The immediate purpose of the Book of Habakkuk is to foretell Judah's punishment and to pronounce doom on the Chaldeans (Babylonians). The deeper purpose is to teach the grand truth that the just shall live by faith.

Habakkuk asked two questions in the first chapter: why does God permit injustice? (1:2-4); and why is God silent when the wicked triumph? (1:12-17). These questions in one form or another have troubled believers from the beginning. Why does God permit the wicked to succeed in this world? Why doesn't he act so that good people rather than the wicked prosper?

The answers we find in Habakkuk show us that the wicked do not ultimately succeed. The Lord responded to Habakkuk's perplexity by saying two things. First, God judges his people when they sin (1:5-11). God has the power to use evil men to accomplish his good purposes. Second, God judges the heathen as they sin (2:2-20). Meanwhile when faced with perplexities the godly must embrace three truths: First, *the just shall live by his faith* (2:4b KJV). Second, *for the earth will be filled with the knowledge of the glory of the LORD, as the waters cover the sea* (2:14). Third, *the LORD is in his holy temple; let all the earth be silent before him* (2:20).

In chapter 3 Habakkuk describes the glory of the Lord's coming to Judah to bring judgment on wayward Israel and on the oppressors of God's people as well. The resolute commitment of Habakkuk to faith in the Lord regardless of circumstances (3:18-19) is a model for believers throughout the centuries.

Thus there is a stark contrast between the way this book begins and the way it concludes. Chapter one consists of interrogation, chapter 3 of affirmation. One might say that the book presents a journey of faith from complaint to confidence, from burden to blessing. In chapter 1 Habakkuk was focused on the problem of evil; in chapter three he focuses on the person of God.

Like Jonah, Habakkuk faced a test of faith. This prophet, however, responded to the test exactly opposite to the way Jonah faced it. Jonah ran from God; Habakkuk ran to God. Both men prayed. Jonah, however, prayed in the midst of trouble while Habakkuk prayed after the time of trouble (ch. 3). In the final scene Jonah is immersed in foolish prejudice; but in the end Habakkuk's faith soared. Jonah's rebellion landed him in a fish; Habakkuk's restlessness drove him to a watchtower (2:4).

Anticipation

There is one personal messianic prophecy in the Book of Habakkuk. This prophet foresees the day when God will come in power to deliver his people. He will crush the leader of the land of wickedness (Satan), piercing him through by his own spear (Habakkuk 3:12-15). When Christ died on the cross and rose victoriously from the grave, he won the victory over Satan.

Keys

The key chapter in the Book of Habakkuk is chapter 3. The last three verses form a triumphant climax to the book. This majestic chapter records in highly poetic language God's intervention in the affairs of men.

The key verse in the book is this: *the righteous will live by his faith* (Habakkuk 2:4b).

Key words in the book include *behold* (6), *woe* (5) and *salvation* (3).

Special Features

Here are some of the things that set Habakkuk apart within the biblical collection.

❖ About two-thirds of this book consists of a dialogue between God and the prophet, initiated by the prophet.

❖ The final chapter of this book is a song of confidence in God. This song was later set to music and sung or recited in worship services.

❖ Three times the New Testament quotes the phrase from Habakkuk that would later launch the Protestant

Reformation: *The righteous will live by his faith* (2:4). See Romans 1:17; Galatians 3:11; Hebrews 10:38.

❖ A legend recorded in the apocryphal *Bel and the Dragon* says that Habakkuk took a bowl of stew to Daniel while he was in the lions' den. An angel reportedly transported him there by the hair of his head.

❖ The earliest commentary on any biblical book was on the Book of Habakkuk. It was found among the Dead Sea Scrolls.

HEAR

Aside from the three verses that were quoted above in God's answer to Habakkuk, these verses are favorites in the book:

❖ *I will stand at my watch, and station myself on the ramparts; I will look to see what he will say unto me, and what answer I am to give to this complaint* (2:1).

❖ *Woe to him who gives drink to his neighbors, pouring it from the wineskin till they are drunk, so that he can gaze on their naked bodies* (2:15).

❖ *Renew them in our day, in our time make them known; in wrath remember mercy* (3:2).

❖ *Although the fig tree does not bud and there are no grapes on the vines, though the olive crop fails and the fields produce no food, though there are no sheep in the pen and no cattle in the stalls, yet I will rejoice in the LORD, I will be joyful in God my Savior* (3:17-18).

36ᵗʰ Bible Book
Book of Zephaniah
Prophet of God's Wrath

The name Zephaniah means *he whom Yahweh has hidden.* Three others in the Old Testament also wear this name. Not much is known about the personal life of the author of this book. We know that he was the son of Cushi, a descendant of good King

Hezekiah. Zephaniah may have been the teacher of the young King Josiah. This might explain why the young boy was so bent on a path of revival and reform during his childhood.

Zephaniah has been called "the orator" (Robinson), "the zealous" (Ward) and "the prophet of all nations" (Scofield). G. Campbell Morgan dubbed him "the prophet of the severity and goodness of God." Zephaniah certainly was the "prophet of the wrath and mercy of God" (Elliott).

The Book of Zephaniah contains three chapters, fifty-three verses, and 1,617 words.

Situation

The political background of Zephaniah is much the same as that of Nahum. The Assyrian Empire was fading. A new power—Babylon—was rising in the east. In Judah the times in which Zephaniah prophesied were rotten. Judah was characterized by self-complacent pride, shameless falsehood, flagrant iniquity, merciless extortion, and senseless idolatry. The guilty transgressors were unabashed. They knew no shame.

Zephaniah prophesied during the reign of King Josiah. The dates generally assigned to Zephaniah are 640 to 609 BC. Perhaps encouraged and directed by Zephaniah, King Josiah launched the last and most thorough reformation in the history of Judah. The reform began in Josiah's eighth year of reign (634 BC), intensified in his twelfth year (630 BC), and reached a climax with the discovery of a lost book of God's law in 621 BC.

Prophets on the scene with Zephaniah were Nahum, Habakkuk, and Jeremiah.

Plan

Zephaniah consists entirely of prophetic oracles arranged in three divisions: the *sin* of Judah (1:1–2:3); the *sentence* against the nations (2:4–3:8), and the *salvation* of the remnant (3:9–20). Zephaniah looks *within* his own country in the first unit, he looks *around* to other nations in the second, and he looks *forward* in the third unit. The first two units portray God's wrath; the third chapter pictures a day of joy.

Eternal Purpose

The immediate purpose of the Book of Zephaniah is to warn Judah of approaching doom. The deeper purpose of the book is to warn hardened sinners about the wrath of God and to give encouragement to those who repent.

The theme of the book is *the day of Yahweh*. Zephaniah emphasizes the imminence (1:2-3; 2:4-15; 3:8), universality (1:14ff.), and terror of that day (1:17). For Zephaniah the coming judgment is the reversal of creation. In Genesis 1 God had created fish, birds, land animals, and human beings, in that order. In the day of wrath God is going to destroy *people and animals, birds and fish* (1:3). In many ways Zephaniah is a fierce and grim book of warning. Desolation, darkness, and ruin will strike Judah and the Gentile nations because of the wrath of God upon sin.

While the book focuses largely on the theme of God's wrath, it does hold out the promise of redemption and salvation for those who believe. Furthermore, Zephaniah looks beyond judgment to a time of joy. In that day God will cleanse the nations and restore the fortunes of his people.

Anticipation

There is no personal messianic prophecy in Zephaniah. The book, however, does anticipate the day when Jews and Gentiles will stand shoulder to shoulder in the kingdom of God (3:9 NIV). This anticipation is fulfilled in the church of Christ where God has removed the barriers that separated the two peoples (Ephesians 2:14).

Keys

The key chapter in the Book of Zephaniah is chapter 3. This chapter makes the point that the day of the Lord involves retribution on sinners and restoration of the saved.

The key verse in the book is this: *the day of the* LORD *is near* (1:7b).

The key phrase in Zephaniah is *in that day* (3).

The key word is *remnant* (4).

Special Features

Here are some special facts that stand out about Zephaniah:

- ❖ Zephaniah is the only prophet of royal descent.
- ❖ Christ alluded to Zephaniah on two occasions: Matthew 13:41 (Zephaniah 1:3); Matthew 24:29 (Zephaniah 1:15).
- ❖ Both Joel and Zephaniah deal almost exclusively with the concept of the coming day of Yahweh. Zephaniah refers to it some twenty-three times.

HEAR

Here are some favorite passages from Zephaniah:

- ❖ *I will sweep away both men and animals; I will sweep away the birds of the air and the fish of the sea* (1:3a)
- ❖ *Then I will purify the lips of the peoples, that all of them may call on the name of the LORD and serve him shoulder to shoulder* (3:9)
- ❖ *The remnant of Israel will do no wrong; they will speak no lies nor will deceit be found in their mouths. They will eat and lie down and no one will make them afraid* (3:13).

CHAPTER FOURTEEN

FOCUS BOOKS (6)
Haggai–Malachi

With this lesson we conclude our survey of the seventeen Focus Books of the Old Testament — the five Major and the twelve Minor Prophets. The final three prophets — Haggai, Zechariah, and Malachi — are sometimes called the *postexilic prophets*. All three ministered in the Persian province of Judea following the return of the Jews from Babylon to their homeland. As we shall see shortly, Haggai and Zechariah worked together; Malachi ministered almost a century later.

37th Bible Book
Book of Haggai
Prophet of Temple Building

The name *Haggai* means *festive or festival*. He is the only person by this name in the Bible. His name is mentioned nine times in the book. Virtually nothing is known about this prophet.

Haggai has been called "the prophet of divine shaking," "the matter-of-fact prophet" (Box), "the master builder" (Ward), and "the prophet of relative values" (Morgan). Perhaps the most picturesque title that has been bestowed upon him is found in the Harper Study Bible: "the goad of God." The sharp-pointed messages of this man were used by God to provoke his people to frenzied action in rebuilding the Temple of the Lord.

The Book of Haggai contains two chapters, thirty-eight verses, and 1,131 words.

Situation

Babylon fell to the armies of Cyrus the Persian in 539 BC. The Jews were then allowed to return to their homeland. They began with great zeal the reconstruction of their Temple, but then discouragement set in. For over fifteen years no further work on the Temple was done. In 520 BC through the preaching of Haggai and Zechariah God encouraged the people to resume construction. The Temple was finally dedicated in 516 BC.

Haggai ministered to those who returned to Judea from Babylon. His ministry was only four months. It is precisely dated between August and December of the year 520 BC. The focus of Haggai's efforts was the rebuilding of God's Temple.

Plan

The Book of Haggai consists of four oracles. In the first Haggai reproved the remnant for failing to complete God's Temple. In the second he offered encouragement to those who resumed the building effort. In the third Haggai pronounced divine blessing on the builders. In the fourth oracle the prophet gave to the people of God assurance of a glorious future. An appealing outline of the book is this:

- ❖ **A Call to Action** (ch. 1)
- ❖ **A Call to Courage** (2:1-9)
- ❖ **A Call to Patience** (2:10-19)
- ❖ **A Call to Hope** (2:20-23)

Aside from Haggai himself, the book alludes to Zerubbabel the governor of the land and Joshua the high priest. Part of Haggai's mission was to encourage these godly men in the Temple-building project.

Eternal Purpose

Haggai's message does not sound like that of prophets prior to the exile. He says nothing about idolatry, nothing about injustice or violence. Haggai's single purpose was to urge the Jews to put God first. They should demonstrate their commitment by finishing construction of the Temple. So the immediate purpose of the Book of Haggai is to encourage the Jews to build God's Temple. One could say that Haggai had a single-track mind. The deeper purpose is to announce the day when the kingdom that cannot be shaken was to emerge.

Haggai's message has an important stewardship application. Financial problems are directly associated with a person's giving to the Lord. The people did not build the Temple because they had no money (1:3-11); they had no money, however, because they did not build the Temple (Proverbs 11:24-25; Malachi 3:10-12).

Another important principle taught in Haggai is that lack of separation from the world is devastating to success in God's work. It results in contamination and ineffectiveness both on the personal and the congregational level (2:13-17).

The short ministry of Haggai illustrates the power of the word of God and the place of preaching in accomplishing God's purposes. Haggai lacks the vivid imagery and poetry of some of his predecessors; but his concise and austere messages were successful.

Haggai was one of the few prophets whose message brought quick and tangible results. Only twenty-three days after his first oracle, the people resumed work on the Temple after a fifteen-year hiatus. In four months Haggai accomplished more than any other Old Testament prophet. He was "a steam-engine in trousers" (Pfeiffer). By the time he retired or died the work of reconstructing the house of God was well under way.

The significance of the Temple in God's program of redemption is generally not appreciated. The Temple was the focus of the whole system of offerings and sacrifices, priests and worship. It was also the symbol of Israel's spiritual identity. The Temple was a visible reminder of the person, power, and presence of God. Now that the throne of David no longer existed, it was especially important that the Temple be rebuilt. The Temple was to serve as a rallying point both to the remnant that had returned to Judea, and to those who remained scattered in foreign lands.

Anticipation

Two passages in Haggai speak directly of the coming of Messiah. The first of these is camouflaged in most English translations. The KJV, however, makes it clear: *I will shake all nations, and the desire of all nations shall come* (2:7). Christ is here called The Desire of All Nations because in him are found all the attributes of a Savior for whom Gentiles yearn. The prophecy in 2:21-23 about Zerubbabel being God's signet in a future unshakable kingdom also has messianic implications. Jesus was descended from Zerubbabel on both his mother's side and his father's. Jesus is the second Zerubbabel!

Keys

The key chapter in the Book of Haggai is chapter 2. This chapter contains startling messianic prophecies about a great shaking of the world, and a kingdom that cannot be shaken.

The key verse in the book is this: *Consider your ways* (1:5 KJV). This challenge appears twice in complete form (1:5, 7) and three additional times in an abbreviated form (2:15, 18). The use of the imperative *be strong* three times in 2:4 also should be noted.

Key phrases in Haggai include: *Zerubbabel the son of Shealtiel, governor of Judah, and Joshua the son of Jehozadak, the high priest* (4), *the word of the LORD came* (5), and *oracle of the LORD* (11).

The key word is *consider* (4).

Special Features

Here are some interesting facts that set Haggai apart within Holy Writ.

❖ Haggai is the first prophet whose message was enthusiastically embraced by God's people and quickly implemented.

❖ Haggai is cited by name in the Book of Ezra as one of the key motivators in arousing the people of Judea to rebuild the Temple (Ezra 5:1; 6:14).

❖ On the basis of 2:3 some have suggested that Haggai may have seen the first Temple in its glory. If so, he was a septuagenarian when he began to prophesy.

❖ Haggai is the second shortest book in the Old Testament.

❖ If his book contains all Haggai's messages, his ministry lasted less than four months.

❖ Haggai must have had a penchant for precise dating, for he reports the month and day for each prophecy as well as the date that the Jews resumed work on the Temple.

❖ Haggai's words ring with divine authority. *Thus says the* Lord and similar expressions appear twenty-six times in thirty-eight verses.

HEAR

God has something to say to us through Haggai. Here are some favorite passages that might whet your appetite for a study of this book.

❖ *Is it a time for you yourselves to be living in your paneled houses, while this house remains a ruin?* (1:4).

❖ *"I am with you," declares the* Lord (1:13).

❖ *In a little while I will once more shake the heavens and the earth, the sea and the dry land* (2:6).

❖ *"The silver is mine and the gold is mine," declares the* Lord *Almighty* (2:8).

❖ *"The glory of this present house will be greater than the glory of the former house," says the* Lord *Almighty. "And in this place I will grant peace," declares the* Lord *Almighty* (2:9).

38th Bible Book
Book of Zechariah
Prophet of Night Visions

The name *Zechariah* means *whom Yahweh remembered*. The name in the Old Testament is quite common. Twenty-seven others have this name. The author of the thirty-eighth book is distinguished from the others by mention of the name of his father (Berechiah) and grandfather (Iddo). Assuming that he is mentioned in Nehemiah 12, this writer was a priest and head of a father's house in the days of Joiakim who succeeded Joshua as high priest (Nehemiah 12:12, 16).

Some think that Jesus alluded to the death of this Zechariah in Matthew 23:35. Others think that Jesus was referring to a namesake of our writer. Cf. Luke 11:51; 2 Chronicles 24:17-22.

Zechariah has been called "the Temple builder" and "the seer" (Robinson). Patterson referred to this prophet as "the idealist" while Ward branded him "the enthusiast." Since such a large part of his book centers on eight visions which he received in one night, Zechariah might appropriately be called "the prophet of night visions."

The Book of Zechariah contains fourteen chapters, 211 verses, and 6,444 words. This is the longest book of the Minor Prophets.

Situation

When Zechariah began to prophesy, Haggai's ministry was winding down. The Temple rebuilding effort was under way. The Persian King Darius was the master of the world.

Zechariah's ministry was among the remnant that returned from captivity. They were living in the vicinity of Jerusalem. Zechariah began to prophesy in late October or early November of 520 BC. On the front end Zechariah's ministry overlaps by a month or so the ministry of Haggai.

Zechariah was on the scene throughout the long reign of the Persian King Darius the Great. He lived to see his own predictions of Temple completion fulfilled in 516 BC. Zechariah probably lived through the period of the Battle of Marathon (490 BC) when the Persians were defeated in an attempt to invade Greece. This may have triggered Zechariah's comments about the coming of the Greeks (9:13). He probably lived into the early years of King Xerxes who began to reign in 486 BC.

Plan

The Book of Zechariah — especially the last six chapters — is one of the most difficult of the prophetic books to interpret. Much here is obscure and difficult to fit into any system of prophetic interpretation. The conflicting interpretations of modern scholars are not just limited to individual words or verses, but to the entire structure of the book.

The Book of Zechariah consists of eight visions with messages connected to each. The book also contains action parables and prophetic oracles unconnected with the visions.

Structural plan. The material has been arranged in two major divisions: messages during the construction of the Temple (chs. 1–6); and messages after the completion of the Temple (chs. 7–14). The first division is written in prose, the second in Hebrew poetry.

A more detailed breakdown of the first division looks like this: introduction (1:1-6), eight visions (1:7-6:8) climaxing in a symbolic crowning of Joshua the high priest (6:9-15). Following a lengthy introduction (chs. 7–8) the second division has a "burden" (chs. 9–10), an action parable (ch. 11), and a second "burden" (chs. 12–14). A *burden* is a weighty prophetic word.

Biographical plan. This book focuses on two individuals besides Zechariah himself: Zerubbabel the governor of Judea and Joshua the high priest.

Geographical plan. The setting for Zechariah is the Persian province of Judea. The prophetic sections of the book speak of Greece, Egypt, Philistia, and indeed the entire world.

The Book of Zechariah in its entirety can be classified as *apocalyptic* literature. This highly figurative type of literature (like the

Book of Revelation) has certain characteristics that distinguish it. For example, the prophetic portrayals of the future progress from the local scene of the writer to the world scene; from a point in time to the end of time. Visions are common. Angels are featured prominently. Apocalyptic literature reflects a certain determinism. God already has worked out his purposes in heaven. All that remains is for him to initiate those purposes on earth. In apocalyptic literature there is an abundance of animal symbolism as well as the use of symbolic numbers.

Eternal Purpose

The immediate purpose of the Book of Zechariah is to encourage the Jews in their Temple building. The deeper purpose of the book is to set forth beautiful foreglimpses of the Messiah and his kingdom.

Like Haggai, Zechariah was concerned about Temple building. There are, however, these differences. Haggai focused on arousing the people to perform an outward task; Zechariah was intent on producing in the people a spiritual change. The scope of Haggai's ministry is limited to the local area around Jerusalem; Zechariah bears a universal message. Haggai's message is short, clear, and specific; Zechariah is long, and somewhat fuzzy because of the number of visions. While Haggai hints at the messianic future, Zechariah gives a detailed picture of that coming day.

Zechariah believed God's Temple must be built, for one day the Messiah would fill it with his glory. Future blessing, however, is contingent upon present obedience. Temple building for Zechariah was not merely a physical construction project; it was a demonstration of faith in the future of God's people. Zechariah urged wholehearted zeal in the work because the building was for their Messiah.

Comparisons are often made between the books of Zechariah and Daniel. Both prophets see the sweep of history from their own days to the final day. Both begin with Gentile domination and end with Christ's dominion. Zechariah, however, goes into a bit more detail on the nature of the kingdom that Christ will rule.

He foresees the day that God's kingdom will be established on the earth, a kingdom of peace, holiness, and worship. Nations that refuse to participate in that kingdom life will not receive the blessing of the Lord. Zechariah depicts the progression of God's people from slavery to salvation, from persecution to peace, from uncleanness to holiness, and from lamentation to jubilation.

Anticipation

In comparison to its size Zechariah contains a greater percentage of personal messianic prophecy than any other book of the Old Testament. This prophet speaks of the coming King and of his kingdom as well. Here are some of the outstanding prophecies pertaining to Christ in Zechariah:

- ❖ **Promise of a new Priest** (3:8-10)
- ❖ **A priest upon his throne** (6:12-13)
- ❖ **Prince of peace** (9:9-11)
- ❖ **Ruler with four titles** (10:4)
- ❖ **Rejected Shepherd** (11:4-14)
- ❖ **Pierced One** (12:10)
- ❖ **Smitten Shepherd** (13:7)

Keys

The key chapter in the Book of Zechariah is chapter 6. This chapter contains the account of the symbolic crowning of Joshua the high priest which has messianic implications.

The key verse in the book is this: *"Not by might nor by power, but by my Spirit," says the* LORD *Almighty* (4:6b).

Key phrases in the book include *the* LORD *Almighty* (52) and *in that day* (20).

Key words include *behold* (22) and *Jerusalem* (41).

Special Features

Here are some distinguishing features of the Book of Zechariah:

- ❖ Zechariah is the largest book of the Minor Prophets. For this reason he has been called the "major Minor Prophet."

❖ According to Jewish tradition, Zechariah was a member of the Great Synagogue that collected and preserved the Scriptures.

❖ Zechariah is second only to Isaiah in the number of messianic prophecies it contains. As to percentage of content Zechariah exceeds Isaiah.

❖ Many of the images in the Book of Revelation originated with Zechariah.

HEAR

Here are some of the outstanding chapters in Zechariah:

❖ Vision of the man with a measuring line (ch. 2)

❖ Vision of the cleansing of Joshua (ch. 3)

❖ Vision of the golden lampstand (ch. 4)

❖ Rejection of the Good Shepherd (ch. 11)

Here are some of the favorite verses from the Book of Zechariah:

❖ *Strike the shepherd, and the sheep shall be scattered* (13:7).

❖ *Rejoice greatly, O daughter of Zion! Shout, daughter of Jerusalem! See, your king comes to you, righteous and having salvation, gentle and riding on a donkey, on a colt, the foal of a donkey* (9:9).

❖ *"Return to me," declares the* LORD *Almighty, "and I will return to you," says the* LORD *Almighty* (1:3).

❖ *Once again men and women of ripe old age will sit in the streets of Jerusalem, each with his cane in hand because of his age. The city streets will be filled with boys and girls playing there* (8:4-5).

❖ *In those days ten men from all languages and nations will take firm hold of one Jew by the hem of his robe and say, "Let us go with you, because we have heard that God is with you* (8:23).

❖ *I told them, "If you think it best, give me my pay; but if not, keep it." So they paid me thirty pieces of silver* (11:12).

❖ *On that day living water will flow out from Jerusalem, half to the eastern sea and half to the western sea, in summer and in winter. ⁹The* LORD *will be king over the whole earth. On that day there will be one* LORD, *and his name the only name* (14:8-9).

❖ *Then the survivors from all the nations that have attacked Jerusalem will go up year after year to worship the King, the* LORD *Almighty, and to celebrate the Feast of Tabernacles* (14:16).

39ᵗʰ Bible Book
Book of Malachi
Prophet of Interrogation

The name *Malachi* means *my messenger.* He is the only person of this name in the Bible. Nothing is known about Malachi.

The Book of Malachi contains four chapters, fifty-five verses, and 1,782 words.

Situation

In 457 BC Ezra was permitted by the Persian King Artaxerxes to return to Jerusalem to enforce the law of God. Apparently Ezra also attempted to rebuild the walls of Jerusalem. He was forced to stop by orders of the king. In 445 BC the same king gave Nehemiah permission to return to rebuild the walls of Jerusalem. Nehemiah served a thirteen-year term as governor, then returned to Shushan or Susa to be recommissioned. He came back to Judea in 432 BC for another term as governor.

Jerusalem in Malachi had just been rebuilt and repopulated. The Temple, however, had been functioning for almost a century. The Persians ruled the world at the time. Their philosophy generally was to grant religious freedom to subject peoples. While some of the neighboring peoples made life difficult for the Jews, for the most part during this period the Jews were free to practice their faith as they saw fit.

Spiritually the Jews of the fifth century had lost the joy of their salvation and their zeal for the Lord. The priesthood was degenerate. The people brought blemished sacrifices, and the priests approved them for presentation before God. Religious apathy and skepticism were widespread. Tithes were neglected. Divorce was common. Yet the people and priests refused to admit that anything was wrong.

Into this environment Malachi marched. With these hypocrites and apostates he engaged in public debate. When he was finished, he had laid bare the rotten foundation upon which their relationship to God rested.

Restored Jerusalem was the scene of Malachi's ministry. He seems to have prophesied during Nehemiah's brief absence from the city in 432 BC.

Plan

The method of this prophet is distinctive. It has been called the dialogue method. Seven times in the book this pattern recurs. Malachi made an affirmation or assertion about some sin or problem in the community. The people then objected to the charge by interrogating Malachi. They demanded in effect that Malachi explain the charge and present his evidence. Thus the dominant pattern in the book is assertion, objection, and refutation. Malachi probes deeply into the problems of his day by making use of this question-and-answer technique. Those problems included hypocrisy, infidelity, mixed marriages, divorce, false worship, and arrogance.

As a poet Malachi does not measure up to the other prophets. The parallelism is less pronounced. The imagery lacks force and beauty. Some have accused him of having a spiritual hardening of the arteries that eventually became widespread in Pharisaism. This charge, however, is grossly unfair. Malachi was not a formalist. His book breathes the genuine prophetic spirit. Here is an incisiveness and insightfulness that is unequaled by any other.

The Book of Malachi falls into two major divisions: *the priests sin against God's love* (1:6–2:9) and *the people sin against God's love* (2:10–4:3). At the outset Malachi presents his grand thesis that Yahweh loves his people even though their circumstances might argue otherwise (1:1-5). The book concludes with a final exhortation (4:4-6).

Eternal Purpose

The immediate purpose of the Book of Malachi is to correct the abuses and attitudes of the Jewish community at the close of the Old Testament period. The deeper purpose is to announce the coming of the Sun of Righteousness and the day when God was to be worshiped throughout the world in spirit and in truth.

Malachi's dialogue style was designed to appeal to thinking people. He decisively answered those who because of disbelief, disappointment, and discouragement challenged his assertions. Malachi was preaching to a people who had concluded that it just did not pay to serve God. This attitude accounts for their moral laxity and religious corruption.

Malachi revealed that God still loved Israel in spite of their lapse of faith and commitment. He wanted the people and priests to realize that their lack of blessing was not caused by God's lack of concern. It was caused by their compromise and disobedience to God's law. Only repentance and reconsecration could remove the barriers to blessing.

Malachi warns believers of all ages not to engage in church games. His words call for a reexamination of our relationship with the Lord. God cannot smile on halfhearted commitment and casual worship that does not recognize the greatness of the Lord (1:14).

Anticipation

Two passages in Malachi qualify as pointing personally to the coming Messiah. In 3:1 Malachi announced the sudden appearance of the Lord. He is the messenger of the covenant, the one who will institute a new covenant. His coming is preceded by another messenger who prepares the way for him. This earlier messenger refers to John the Baptist.

In the second passage Malachi referred to the Messiah as the *Sun of Righteousness* (4:2). His coming will signal a new day of healing, joy, and triumph for God's people.

In addition, Malachi heralds the day when the Lord will be sincerely worshiped worldwide (1:11, 14). He also announces the appearance of Elijah before the coming of the great and dreadful day of the Lord (4:5). The reference again is to John the Baptist (Matthew 11:14; 17:12).

Keys

The key chapter in the Book of Malachi is chapter 3. This chapter contains the dramatic prophecies of the coming of Christ and John the Baptist.

The key verse in the book is this: *Will a man rob God? Yet you rob me* (3:8a). This book rebukes the Judeans for withholding from God his just due.

The key phrase is this: *you say* (10).

The key word in Malachi is *curse/cursed* (6).

Special Features

Here are some of the distinguishing features of the final book of the Old Testament:

- ❖ In the Hebrew Bible the verses of this book are divided into only three chapters.
- ❖ In this book Malachi answers eight questions by which his audience challenged his accusations against them.
- ❖ Malachi's prediction of the coming of Elijah (4:5) is the basis for a custom of setting a place for Elijah—the so-called Elijah cup—at the Jewish Passover Seder. Jews also leave the door ajar for Elijah to enter and join in their celebration.
- ❖ Many scholars think that *malachi* (*my messenger*) is a descriptive title rather than a proper name. Some ancient writers attributed this book to Ezra.
- ❖ Of the fifty-five verses in the book, forty-seven are spoken by God.
- ❖ Malachi is the only prophet who ends his book with judgment. The last word of the Old Testament is *curse*.

HEAR

Here are some of the favorite passages from the Book of Malachi:

❖ *But for you who revere my name, the sun of righteousness will rise with healing in its wings. And you will go out and leap like calves released from the stall* (4:2).

❖ *Have we not all one father? Did not one God created us? Why do we profane the covenant of our fathers by breaking faith with one another?* (2:10).

❖ *"I hate divorce," says the* LORD *God of Israel* (2:16).

❖ *Then those who feared the* LORD *talked with each other, and the* LORD *listened and heard. A scroll of remembrance was written in his presence concerning those who feared the* LORD *and honored his name* (3:16).

❖ *See, I will send you the prophet Elijah before that great and dreadful day of the* LORD *comes* (4:5).

Unfortunately it seems that the words of Malachi had little impact on the Judeans. This was God's last effort to reach his people through heaven-sent messengers for four hundred years. God remained silent during the period between the Old and New Testaments. Only with the coming of John the Baptist (3:1) did God again communicate to his people through a prophet's voice. It was John's glorious privilege to announce that the kingdom of heaven was at hand (Matthew 3:2).

The final paragraph of Malachi is a fitting conclusion to the Old Testament. Here the prophet reaches back in time to embrace the Law of Moses. He stretches forward in time to embrace Messiah's forerunner. He thus forges a link between the law and the gospel, the Old Testament and the New.

Appendix

Christ in Every Book

Every book of the Old Testament has a link to Christ. Sometimes that link is stated in bold, specific prophecy. Other times it is inferred from the contents of the book as a whole.

In Genesis he's the Promised Seed.
In Exodus he's the Passover Lamb.
In Leviticus he's the Perfect Priest.
In Numbers he's Balaam's Star and Scepter.
In Deuteronomy he's the Prophet like unto Moses.

In Joshua he's the Captain of our Salvation.
In Judges he's the Final Deliverer.
In Ruth he's our Kinsman-Redeemer.
In Samuel he's David's Son who Rules forever.
In Kings he is the King of all kings.
In Chronicles he's the Greater temple.

In Job he's the Redeemer of the Last Days.
In Psalms he's the Enthroned Priest-King.
In Proverbs he is Wisdom Personified.
In Ecclesiastes he is the Supreme Good.
In Song of Solomon he is Fairest of Ten Thousand.

In Isaiah he's the Virgin-born Child and Suffering Servant.
In Jeremiah he's Mediator of the New Covenant.

In Lamentations he's the One who Weeps over Jerusalem.
In Ezekiel he's the Good Shepherd.
In Daniel he's One like a Son of Man who ascends to the Father.

In Hosea he's the Second Moses, David, and Israel.
In Joel he's the Teacher for Righteousness.
In Amos he's the Restorer of the Tent of David.
In Obadiah he's the Deliverer on Mount Zion.
In Jonah he's the Resurrected Prophet.
In Micah he's the Ruler from Bethlehem.
In Nahum he's Avenger of his People.
In Habakkuk he's Victor over the Ruler of Darkness.
In Zephaniah he's the Purifier of Zion.
In Haggai he's the Desire of all Nations.
In Zechariah he's the Rejected Shepherd.
In Malachi he's the Sun of Righteousness and
Messenger of the Covenant.

OTHER BOOKS BY THE AUTHOR

Available from College Press, Joplin, Mo. www.collegepress.com
  The Pentateuch, 1993, 534 pp.
  The Books of History, 1995, 747 pp.
  The Wisdom Literature and Psalms, 1996, 873 pp.
  The Major Prophets, 1992, 637 pp.
  The Minor Prophets, 1994, 653 pp.
  1 & 2 Samuel in "The College Press NIV Commentary," 2000. 541 pp.
  Bible History Made Simple, 2009, 180 pp.
  New Testament Books Made Simple, 2009, 177 pp.

Also by this author:
  What the Bible Says about the Promised Messiah 1991, 522 pp.
  Biblical Protology, 2007, 530 pp.
  Postexilic Prophets, 2007, 268 pp.
  Daniel: a Christian Interpretation, 2008, 416 pp.
  Ezekiel: a Christian Interpretation, 2008, 468 pp.
  Jeremiah: a Christian Interpretation, 2008, 540 pp.

For articles and commentaries and other materials, check the author's web site: bibleprofessor.com